Being Moved
by Moving Words

Westar Studies

The Westar Studies series offers distinctive scholarly publications on topics related to the field of Religious Studies. The studies seek to be multi-dimensional both in terms of the subject matter addressed and the perspective of the author. Westar Studies are not related to Westar seminars but offer scholars a deliberate space of free inquiry to engage both scholarly peers and the public.

Being Moved by Moving Words

*Crediting Rhetoric in the Theopoetics
of John D. Caputo*

JOSEPH BESSLER

Foreword by Arthur J. Dewey

CASCADE *Books* · Eugene, Oregon

BEING MOVED BY MOVING WORDS
Crediting Rhetoric in the Theopoetics of John D. Caputo

Westar Studies

Copyright © 2025 Joseph Bessler. All rights reserved. Except for brief quotations in critical publications or reviews, no part of this book may be reproduced in any manner without prior written permission from the publisher. Write: Permissions, Wipf and Stock Publishers, 199 W. 8th Ave., Suite 3, Eugene, OR 97401.

Cascade Books
An Imprint of Wipf and Stock Publishers
199 W. 8th Ave., Suite 3
Eugene, OR 97401

www.wipfandstock.com

PAPERBACK ISBN: 978-1-5326-0889-6
HARDCOVER ISBN: 978-1-5326-0890-2
EBOOK ISBN: 978-1-5326-3709-4

Cataloguing-in-Publication data:

Names: Bessler, Joseph, author. | Dewey, Arthur J., foreword.

Title: Being moved by moving words : crediting rhetoric in the theopoetics of John D. Caputo / Joseph Bessler with a foreword by Arthur J. Dewey.

Description: Eugene, OR: Cascade Books, 2025. | Westar Studies. | Includes bibliographical references and index.

Identifiers: ISBN 978-1-5326-0889-6 (paperback). | ISBN 978-1-5326-0890-2 (hardcover). | ISBN 978-1-5326-3709-4 (ebook).

Subjects: LCSH: Caputo, John D.—Criticism, interpretation, etc. | Religion—Philosophy. | Hermeneutics. | Postmodernism. | Theology. | Rhetoric.

Classification: BT83.597 B39 2025 (print). | BT83.597 (ebook).

VERSION NUMBER 02/12/25

[Scripture quotations are from] New Revised Standard Version Bible, copyright © 1989 National Council of the Churches of Christ in the United States of America. Used by permission. All rights reserved worldwide.

I am using *The Complete Gospels: The Scholars Version* (SV) to translate the Greek *basileia* as "Empire" of God" rather than "Kingdom of God" to better capture the imperial context in which the New Testament texts were written.

"This very impressive, well-written work is a two-for-one book. It engages John Caputo's stimulating contribution—his metanoetics and his call for transformation, to step out for justice. But it also presents Joe Bessler's fine proposal. He walks along with Caputo 'but not,' magnifying a turn to rhetoric, not as rouge or decoration, but as the 'fine and useful art of making things matter,' as nothing less than being moved to renew the world. Compelling.

—**WARREN CARTER**, Meinders Professor of New Testament, Phillips Theological Seminary, Tulsa, Oklahoma

"In *Being Moved by Moving Words*, Joseph Bessler not only offers a review of the theological thinking of John D. Caputo but also offers a way of thinking theologically with Caputo. Bessler helps us understand, or perhaps understand anew, the moving power of theological rhetoric, which is the power of laughter, the power of compassion, and the power of thinking the unthought. With moving words, Bessler shows us the rhetoric that Caputo holds in spades, and the reader is challenged to take theology out of the mind and have it live in the heart.

—**DAVID GALSTON**, executive director, Westar Institute

"Insightful, illuminating, a pleasure to read these moving words about being moved by moving words. This important and timely book brings us up to date on the crucial linguistic turn in rhetoric and theology from certainty to uncertainty. This counter move returns us to experience the power of language; more evocative, transformative, and compelling than the blunt language of power and coercive argumentation. Joe Bessler brings to us a thoughtful and loving analysis of the groundbreaking radical theology of Jack Caputo and insists that rhetoric understood as poetic discourse and theology as a theopoetics are deeply linked in their mutual commitment and manner to 'the useful art of making things matter.' Bessler affirms the power of moving words to open and engage our imagination, stir our irrepressible response to an authentic call, and move us to act. This is a hopeful book. We will see with new eyes and hear anew how the moving words of rhetoric and theology, now understood as call and response, bring you the reader into urgent and necessary play as we move into an uncertain future. Take up and read this book. And let it move you. It will."

—**MARIANNE BORG**, founder, The Marcus J. Borg Foundation

"Reading this remarkable book, I am reminded that Kierkegaard said, 'Some things are true when whispered but become false when shouted.' John Caputo has dared to whisper about a 'weak' God in a world drunk on the idolatry of power. Now Joe Bessler has brilliantly analyzed the role that rhetoric plays in Caputo's radical theology. Read it, and you will want to shout 'theopoetically' from the rooftops."

—**ROBIN R. MEYERS**, author of *Saving God from Religion*

For Laura

There is no Big Being out there, no Big Book, no Big Institutional Body to back it [Weak Theology] up. Its force is weak, its voice reduced to the whisper of the persuasiveness of what it has to say . . . It lays down the sword of the absolutes—the inerrant books and infallible decrees—that confessional theology carries at its side, in favor of peace, of the weak force of what it has to say.

—JOHN D. CAPUTO.[1]

---

1. Caputo, "A Short Precis," 2–3.

Contents

Foreword by Arthur J. Dewey | ix
Preface | xiii
Acknowledgments | xvii
Abbreviations | xix

Introduction | 1
1 Can I Get an Amen? | 9
2 Mark 3:1–6: No *nous* is Good News | 24
3 Kierkegaard and the Passions of a Scrivner | 30
4 *Nous, Kardia, Phronesis, Oh, My!* | 39
5 Drawing Us In and Calling Us Out | 48
6 The Shape of a Call That Moves Us | 56
7 Disrupting the Play of Hermeneutics | 80
8 Confession | 88

Appendix I: Hearing Footsteps: A Brief Look at Poetics and Rhetoric in the Time of Caputo | 93
Appendix II: "Why Are These the Topics?" A Political and Theological Response | 98
Appendix III: Note on Theopoetics and Rhetoric | 104
Bibliography | 107
Index | 111

Foreword

Twice in my life books, still unpublished, have come to my rescue. More than twenty years ago, returning home from a meeting in Boston, I walked through the nearly deserted airport in Cincinnati. During my flight, the bombing of Baghdad had begun and scenes of devastation played on abandoned TV's as I made my way to baggage. Upon reaching home, my despondent mood was broken by a plain brown package. Walter Wink had sent his second volume on the Powers to me for comment. Little did he know that the manuscript of the non-violent vision of Jesus sustained me for the next two weeks.

More recently, opinions from the Supreme Court continued to undermine the prospect of democracy for our land. And, in the midst of what seemed to me to be a grim prospect for our collective future, Joe Bessler emailed his latest draft of *Being Moved by Moving Words*. In a time of political belligerence and legal disaster, I was challenged to remember not the power plays rushing mindlessly through social media but the weak and wild intimations that were all but overlooked. Joe slowed me down and did so by engaging in a most adventuresome conversation.

Bessler himself admits that he has been taken in by the whisperings he has detected in the work of John Caputo. Indeed, Bessler was not content to simply analyze Caputo's thought. For that would have actually demonstrated that he did not understand what Caputo was about. Rather, Bessler draws on and draws out Caputo's maverick enterprise. He has touched the nerve of Caputo's effort and extended its ramifications into the public domain.

There is a tragic possibility inherent in Caputo's work. Many will read him as a philosopher or even as a theologian. They will be moved by a writer who is also a poet, who has realized the fragile and revelatory aspect of words. He is a thinker who can ski on the margin of meaning and nothingness. And engagement with this bristling thinker will be memorable. But, there are some who would contend that it all stops when the book is placed back on the shelf. Caputo's entire corpus would argue against this. His engagement in areas few philosophers would enter certainly signals this. For Caputo courageously explores the outskirts of language to give his audience the opportunity to detect and play with the deepest echoes of the cosmos.

Here is where Bessler makes such a crucial contribution. Alert to the ranges of Caputo's endeavor, Bessler makes the case that Caputo's insight has an existential public dimension. Bessler does not buy the platitudinous blather about rhetoric; instead, aware of significant advances in rhetorical theory, Bessler, the rhetorical midwife, sensitively delivers Caputo right into the laps of those who will labor along. Caputo wants his readers to realize that life is truly lived in response, that the heart dives deeper in any conversation, that the cry for justice far outdistances the law. Bessler underscores this by showing how each of us is entangled "all the way down," not in a head-trip, but as a matter of the heart. In fact, a rhetorical approach aids us in recognizing that our political options are still open and that we are left to invent what we hope out world can be. It is true one could ignore or walk away from the whisperings at the depth of our life together. We could simply admit how weak and unimportant it all seems, and yet, somehow, something still beckons to action, something seeming so precious invites. . .

Confiteor tibi. Dear Reader, let me conclude with another confession to you. Allow me to put this effort to listen and to enter the public conversation in words I wrote on the edge of things:

> If fingers could forget and yet play on
> or melodies were mastered by the bone,
> if only that there were no need to start
> again the exercises of the chart,
> but wishes will not sing unless they shout
> and blow the heart to let the old stops out.
> And so I play with hands that contradict.
> The organist in church without a sect
> rehearses old devotionals in doubts.
> Where is the sound that gathers up my thoughts
> composing me on a beginning's theme:

is love within the octave of the dream?
Oh, move your eyes on notes across this face
and play my faithless fugue with all your grace.

Arthur J. Dewey
Cincinnati OH Winter 2024

Preface

HE SAYS HIMSELF THAT he could "rightfully pass for an atheist." So, you can understand why I need to begin by confessing my weakness for the theology of John Caputo. The truth is, I have been moved by his work more forcefully than I, as a seminary professor, should have been. I suspect I could easily have avoided this temptation, this late-have-I-read-Thee affection, seeing that I am now somewhat late in my professional career. But I feel compelled to confess that I experienced in my reading of his works something completely unexpected, what can only be called the event of a call, that is to say, of hearing a call in my reading of his writing. Something, I'm not sure what, surprised and spoke to something in me, as if I had been longing and waiting, and in a sense, haunted from a long way away, by this call. To be clear, when I first picked up his work, I did not know Jack well at all. He was outside my conversational orbit—and I could not have anticipated the way his work would move me.

In *The Weakness of God*, as well as in other texts, Caputo crafts a deeply moving proposal that rhymes with and deepens my interests and commitments. While he reimagines *theo-logos* as *theo-poetics*, embracing both the uncertainty and the creativity of all things theological, I find the "forcefulness" of his work to be entwined, or entangled, with my interests in the work of rhetoric, which is, as theorist Thomas B. Farrell says, "the fine and useful art of making things matter."[1]

---

1. See Farrell, "The Weight of Rhetoric," 160.

In these pages, I will seek at once, to walk in Caputo's path, but not.[2] Finding in his work a call that moves me in a very similar yet different direction, I seek, through my attention to his theological proposals to offer something of a "counterpath" to his emphasis on hermeneutics, or interpretation—insisting instead that rhetoric, out of its own deep listening, calls to hermeneutics and presses it to action in public life.[3] Rhetoric, I will suggest, is the public, prophetic push to Caputo's hermeneutics, the call insisting to be spoken out loud.

In place of the language of dogma, which encourages silence and obedience, Caputo urges an understanding of faith as a response that critically and actively engages the world. He sides, for example, with Meister Eckhart in praising Martha more than Mary. He sees in the latter's otherworldliness a form of hiding from the trouble of the world.

> The pulse of radical theology is taken by whether it has an impulse for the world, the stomach for flesh, the spine or heart—I multiply as many *carno*-corporeal animal images as possible—to displace the logos of two worlds, to transfer the funds of its heavenly treasures to earthly accounts.[4]

While I am not imitating Caputo's *theopoetics*, I am attempting to "respond" to him, in the way Jacques Derrida suggests in a conversation with Gary A. Olson on the topic of "rhetoric and composition." Derrida speaks of his writing as a practice of responding.

> I won't say I imitate—that's certainly not true—but I try to match in my own idiom the style or way of writing of the writers I write on. . . . It's not a mimetic behavior but I try to produce my own signature in relation to the signature of the other, . . . it's a listening to the other and trying to produce your own style in proportion to the other.[5]

In this volume, I will focus primarily but by no means solely, on Caputo's works, *The Weakness of God*, and *The Insistence of God*. Across the range of his scholarly production, Caputo longs for his readers to listen and respond, not so much to him, if I can put it that way, but, to the possible event of a call, an event that might happen in their reading of his work, a call that

---

2. Caputo, *What Would Jesus Deconstruct?* 42–46.
3. Caputo, *What Would Jesus Deconstruct?*, 55.
4. Caputo, *Insistence of God*, 65.
5. Olson, "Jacques Derrida," 5.

might interrupt and break open their embedded assumptions about human and divine power and what it means to keep the faith and *do* theology.⁶

Even as Caputo himself listens and responds he invents forceful, productive proposals that he hopes can call and perhaps move "us," his readers, into action. To use his words, I want to "suture" or "wire-up" his language of interpretation, of "hermeneutics all the way down," with my understanding of rhetoric that calls us not simply into but also, in a sense, out of hermeneutics and into the forcefulness of decision and public action. It is not an either/or choice between the two that I am proposing. Rather, I am calling attention to the importance of rhetoric on behalf of the poetic imagination that Caputo uses to open up the transformative work of the discipline that used to be called theology. To put it another way, when one asks, "what's going on in the works of Jack Caputo?" I believe that one potentially helpful way of answering that question is by showing how he puts together his *theopoetic* proposal.

---

6. In his essay, "Foucault's Rhetorical Practice: The 1961 Preface to History and Madness," 145, Michael Ure writes of Foucault: "Like ancient philosophers, in the tradition of philosophy as a way of life, I argue Foucault wrote to inspire in his readers an experience of what Pierre Hadot called conversion or transformation. 'In all its forms,' Hadot explains, 'philosophical conversion is the tearing away from and breaking with the everyday, the familiar, the falsely 'natural' attitude of common sense.' . . . Borrowing Hadot's terms, I identify with Foucault's notion of 'limit-experience' as a type of philosophical conversion that is closer to the pole of rupture, or dramatic change of the subject's being."

Acknowledgments

I WISH TO BEGIN BY thanking President Nancy Pittman and the Board of Trustees at Phillips Theological Seminary for their encouragement across several sabbatical leaves that have enabled me to both research and shape this project that would not let me go. For their personal and institutional support, I am deeply grateful. As I begin my thirty-third year at Phillips, I rejoice for years of creative work with faculty colleagues and students who have changed my life in many ways over the years and continue to do so.

It was David Galston, Director of the Westar Institute, who invited Jack Caputo to participate in, and really, help lead Westar's God Seminar in 2013. Apart from that scholarly and very collegial setting, I would not have met Jack, much less become familiar with his prophetic and creative scholarship.

MaryAnn Morris, former Dean of Students at Phillips, and my writing coach over the past several years, helped me stay on track, even when I wasn't always moving forward. Her critical questions and insights as well as her sense of what was working on the page and what was not proved incredibly helpful. Others who read portions of the manuscript at various stages, including former Phillips President, Gary Peluso Verdend, New Testament colleagues Brandon Scott and Warren Carter, as well as New Testament scholar, Arthur Dewey, and Rev. Marianne Borg, offered suggestions and shared critically helpful responses that kept calling me to listen better to the work I had underway. They frequently heard better than I the turns that I had either missed or needed to make. Many thanks as well to Dean Lisa Davison for her encouragement and interest in the project along with my colleague, church historian Lisa Barnett who has been finishing her own book project this year. Thanks for sharing the journey!

Finally, first, I wish to thank Jack Caputo for his generous hospitality as I have sought to understand and engage his work in a genuinely productive way. Getting to know him through the work of the God Seminar has been a real joy and gift in my life. While my emails weren't exactly knocking on his door at midnight, he kept answering even though he had no idea what to expect from someone interested in the study of rhetoric of all things. His openness to this conversation has meant the world to me as we have moved from strangers to friends.

Finally, second, my life partner, Laura Dempsey, has been with me in times and places where no one else goes. Places of self-doubt, as well as places of celebration; places of anxiety and exhaustion when I had lost the thread of my attention to the work. Her persistent encouragement tempered, at points, with her very frank turns of phrase regarding the pace of my progress, has been a gift, an act of love. I dedicate this book to her.

Abbreviations

NRSV   New Revised Standard Version
SV   Scholar's Version
EI   Emmanuel Levinas, *Ethics and Infinity*
OTB   Emmanuel Levinas, *Otherwise than Being: Or, Beyond Essence*

Introduction

IN THE FOLLOWING PASSAGE from his book *The Weakness of God: A Theology of the Event*, John Caputo identifies himself and his interests with an expansiveness of discourse beyond the walls of authority and self-protection.

> I am interested in displacing distinctions between believer and infidel, theist and atheist, the subscriber to a particular confession and everybody else. We are all in this weak theology together, all exposed to the event under whatever name, all afloat on rafts large and small on an endless sea, all wondering who we are and what is what and who is calling and what is being called for in the name of God.[1]

In these lines, Caputo includes a wide diversity of possible readers, not the usual suspects of confessional traditions, i.e., true believers and theists, but a wider audience, drawn from the margins: "atheists," and "infidels," "all," he says, "in this weak theology together." Yet, Caputo is simultaneously inviting some and disinviting others, the latter being those who seek to exploit the dichotomies of insider and outsider, "center" and "margins," "theist," and "atheist," etc., in the interests of cultural, theological, or political power.

Caputo realizes that in saying out loud and in public that there is no "Big Being," no "Big Book," no "Big Institution," no point of origin or foundational ground to stand on, his proposal of weak theology may not "have a prayer" of acceptance within the church, within the guild of theology, or

---

1. Caputo, *Weakness of God*, 20.

even a yet more public audience. Yet, if there is in these lines a very real sense of chosen, personal vulnerability, one can also hear the edge of one who is "speaking up" against the odds, against the "stronger," more powerful proclamations of institutional authority. Yet, how is such an impossible discourse to proceed?

Might there be, Caputo seems to wonder, a contemporary audience that views the certainty of traditional truths, doctrines, and dogmas of Christianity as the problem? Might there be an audience willing to consider such a proposed indictment of traditional, established power, and perhaps open to risking a public protest that stands up and speaks out for all who have been pushed to the margins? Caputo is not sure there is, but being sure is not the point.

Says rhetorical theorist Thomas B. Farrell about the kind of fundamental changes Caputo seeks: "to challenge and change the normative content in any system of criteria is, of course, a distinctly rhetorical undertaking."[2] And he could add as well: a dangerous one. Moving beyond wondering, Caputo wagers that such an audience, with such convictions, is evident in contemporary North American life and politics. Here, the spiritual and the political begin to weave together, and an audience of resistance informed by a commitment to the unconditionality of justice begins to emerge. And here, we begin to hear Farrell's understanding of rhetoric, "as the fine and useful art of making things matter."[3] In sync more with Richard Vatz's response to Lloyd Bitzer's classic essay, "The Rhetorical Situation," which underscored the role of rhetoric as a "responding discipline," Farrell's emphasis on "making things matter," agrees with Vatz that no "situation" exists before the "intervention of an intending and interpreting speaker subject," or as Caputo would say, "no *event* happens without the intervention of a call." For Vatz and Farrell, rhetorical discourse is "an act of creativity . . . an interpretive art."[4]

To the extent that Caputo already counts on some portion of his potential readers being anti-hierarchical, affirming the full humanity and full participation of those with disabilities, of women, of LGBTQ+, Black and Brown, Yellow, and Red persons, he is already playing off something like Farrell's notion of "social knowledge," or C.W. Tindale's open language of "cognitive environments."[5] Even as Caputo articulates a theological/

2. Farrell, "The Weight of Rhetoric," 478.
3. Farrell, "The Weight of Rhetoric," 160.
4. See Barbara Biesecker, "Rethinking the Rhetorical Situation from within the Thematics of *Différance*," 113.
5. See Farrell, *Norms of Rhetorical Culture*, 265; on "cognitive environments;" see Rieger, "Figuring the Topos: Finding Common Ground, 33–35.

theopoetic proposal that he hopes will speak to others and open within them a space of hearing and response, he cannot be certain his words will reach them. Hence, the radical awareness of his vulnerability, adding the words "if I have any" immediately after mentioning his "readers." He hopes, longs, and prays, that his readers will hear within his pages a call to step out into public life and risk standing for, and calling for, justice. About other "readers," however, he is less welcoming: "If you do not have the least idea of what that [i.e., discussion of the name of "God"] means you would probably be better served to stop reading and check the stock market page to see how your portfolio is doing."[6]

Behind his humor, Caputo's dismissal demonstrates his awareness that some will be more disposed to respond enthusiastically to his proposal than others. And with his image of the "stock-market page" he plays to the trope of the self-centered business type who couldn't be bothered by *kardia* or phrases like "the event of a promise." Their own "portfolio" is as deep as they get.

As an enthusiastic reader of Caputo's work, I clearly belong to the first group. But insofar as I am fascinated with how Caputo both engages his readers and crafts a distinctive proposal for opening up the discourse of theology as it moves into an uncertain future, I explore here how Caputo's *theopoetics* enacts a shift that Dilip Parameshwar Gaonkar calls an "implicit rhetorical turn." By that, he means

> those texts whose authors, while relatively unaware of the rhetorical lexicon, seem to be groping for a vocabulary that could adequately characterize the tropological and suasory aspects of the discursive practices that remain occluded from disciplinary consciousness.[7]

To read Caputo's vibrant texts is to experience someone quite consciously "groping for a vocabulary" that can carry the weight of his innovative moves.[8]

The "locus classicus" of the implicit turn that Gaonkar describes is Thomas Kuhn's *The Structure of Scientific Revolutions*.[9] He writes:

---

6. Caputo, *Weakness of God*, 113.

7. Gaonkar, "Rhetoric and its Double," 203.

8. For Caputo's use of groping or grasping language with respect to the topic of God, see *Weakness*, 287.

9. Besides Kuhn, Gaonkar includes in his list of scholars who "evince signs" of this implicit rhetorical turn: "Paul Feyerabend's *Against Method*, Stephen Toulmin's *The Uses of Argument*, Lacan's *Ecrits*, Gadamer's *Truth and Method*, Foucault's *Archeology of Knowledge*, and Habermas' *The Legitimation Crisis*," to name a few." About these texts, he writes: "These are the master texts of our time, and they are, we're told, bristling with rhetorical insights, even though they often are not consciously recognized." (203)

> The reasons for the choice of this text are quite obvious . . . [i]t brings to light the rhetorical aspect of discursive practices internal to the scientific language community . . . Kuhn makes these profound observations without the slightest awareness of the rhetorical lexicon. [And] . . . though unconscious of rhetoric, he makes a fairly radical claim for the primacy of rhetoric when he asserts that 'paradigm shifts' in any scientific community are more like religious conversions than carefully considered and well-reasoned shifts in scientific practices.[10]

When Caputo calls for a "paradigm shift," analogous to Kuhn's, he uses the Greek word, *metanoia*, to name it, which means "to turn around." The term he coins, *metanoetics*, combines "*metanoia*," (to turn around) with "poetics" (from *poein*, to make) yielding a poetics of transformation. Caputo insists on moving the discipline of theology away from the alleged certainty of dogmatics and metaphysics and embracing, instead, the language of uncertainty—of "perhaps," of "suppose," even of "persuasion," which holds opens the possibility of acting and living differently.

While Caputo's turn to rhetoric is implicit, as Gaonkar suggests, I seek to make Caputo's rhetorical turn more explicit in these pages. For even as he seeks, at one level, to minimize his authorial presence so that his readers might be moved, might experience the encounter of a call, through the very forcefulness of his weak poetics, at another level his leading language of prayers and tears, of being moved, of being called, constructs the poetic contours of an impossible/possible figure that does not exist but *lures* us into existence for others. Given that forcefulness, I share rhetorical scholar, Barbara Biesecker's concern about the tendency to overlook, avoid, and sidestep the significance of rhetoric in contemporary, postmodern discussions of social transformation, such as Caputo's. She writes:

> In the wake of Saussurean and post-Saussurean linguistics it is with an eye to language that radical theorists have begun to critique, revise, and reformulate their understanding of social relations and the agents who constitute and are constituted by them. It is not without consequence, however, that the heightened sensitivity to language has not been coupled with an increased attention to rhetoric. It is remarkable indeed that rhetoric, understood as the art of persuasion, is rarely even mentioned by those theorists and critics most occupied with social transformation.[11]

---

10. Gaonkar, "Rhetoric and its Double," 203.
11. Biesecker, *Addressing Postmodernity*, 3–4.

Biesecker names my concern that something is being more than overlooked in Caputo's suspicion of the vocabulary of argument, debate, proposal, and rhetoric.[12] Something is being silenced. While Caputo seeks in *Weakness* and in *Insistence* to move theology from its centuries-old preoccupation with *hard logical* arguments and unquestionable truth claims, his inclination to silence the language of "debate," "argumentation," and even "proposal," from his model of "weak" theology, goes too far. Instead, he should seek a middle ground, a *tertium quid*, as he likes to say, with room for the play of *logos* with *pathos* and *ethos*.

On this point, Christian Kock, writing in the journal *Philosophy and Rhetoric*, takes issue with the common assumption that rhetoric and argumentation are simply debating "whether some proposition is true."

> In practical reasoning, including rhetorical argumentation, the theme of our reasoning is not a proposition but a proposal to make a deliberate choice—what Aristotle calls a *proairesis* (choice). This is not a proposition expressing a belief or an opinion. Hence it is not something that could be either true or false.[13]

It is the sense of choice, or volition, that suggests the domain of rhetoric is not simply interested in issues of the mind but of the heart. If what is at stake in the moves of a rhetorical argument is not a proposition, or doctrine, but a proposal calling us to decision, to action, and the reorientation of our lives, then attending to how the moves of such a proposal function to call us to respond with our whole hearts, is worth our study, especially of Caputo's rich, transformative discourse.

By using Caputo's work as something of a case study in the failure of crediting rhetoric—especially given his many rhetorical gifts—I hope to enrich the study of Caputo's many contributions that call theology out of a past too given to dogmatic certainties and into an uncertain future that requires courageous engagement, including the acknowledgment of rhetoric as a genuinely creative force that calls forth new proposals—proposals not opposed to *theopoetics* but seeking, as Caputo himself says, in *What Would Jesus Deconstruct*, to "put some teeth"[14] into that very terminology.

12. While Biesecker holds open the possibility that philosophers of the last several generations might have been more schooled in literary theory during their studies than in rhetoric, such an oversight might be corrected by attending to *rhetorical* scholars who have found in Lévinas and Derrida resources for re-imagining and freeing rhetoric from the assumptions of metaphysical stability, in a way similar to Caputo's commitment to free theology from those constraints. See my discussion of Diane Davis' work in chapter seven.

13. Kock, "Defining Rhetorical Argumentation," 445 (emphasis added).

14. Caputo, *What Would Jesus Deconstruct*, 56.

CHAPTER OVERVIEW

In my opening chapter, I try to capture the rhetorical impossibility of convincing a people or a culture, to wish for a "weak God," because it is that very impossibility that Caputo embraces as his starting point for challenging traditional Christian theology's confident proclamation of an all-powerful deity. Having established the significance of "weakness" as a strategic cutting against the language of power, I then begin to explore how Caputo enacts the expansion of his proposal, setting side-by-side two columns of key words and phrases that he associates with the terms "strong theology" and "weak theology, respectively—locating words like "debate," "argument," and "proposal" within the umbrella of strong theology, while locating the language of "poetics" within the field of weak theology.[15]

As he turns away from classical and modern theology's emphasis on "hard arguments," and "formal logic," Caputo acknowledges that he needs those former constructions in a parasitic way. That is to say, for example, we "know" what is weak by "knowing" what is "strong," and *vice versa*. Tracing how Caputo develops his interactive play, both *within* each of the two sets of terms/images, and in the movement *between* them, we will begin to see how this play of words shapes a theological proposal that puts aside Christian theology's traditional dependence upon both Neo-Platonism and modern philosophical worldviews. In the process, Caputo risks a genuinely postmodern proposal for understanding the ongoing work of theology, which he suggests we now call *theopoetics*.

In chapter two, I pick up the interactive tension between the terms "strong" and "weak," and focus on the relation that Caputo creatively develops within those two columns—not just between strong and weak, but now between reason (*logos*) and feeling or passion (*kardia*). Specifically, I explore his treatment, in *Weakness*, of the brief New Testament story, "The Man with a Withered Hand," situated near the beginning of Mark's gospel. In his treatment of the text, Caputo argues that Jesus' confrontation with the Pharisees enacts the tension between strong and weak, head and heart, which he has begun to develop. What Caputo overlooks is Mark's obvious use of miracles, *as an argument,* throughout the three stories of chapter two. Rather than ignore the category of argument and debate, I suggest that Caputo might use these stories to demonstrate a deeper linkage between the poetic and the rhetorical.

In chapter three, I turn from scripture to tradition, examining Caputo's deep affiliation with Søren Kierkegaard, and the latter's strategies of writing

---

15. Hereafter, strong and weak theology.

and reading. Specifically, I argue that Caputo attempts to enact in his writing the kind of authorial non-presence—a non-authorial author—that he finds in Kierkegaard's prose. Playing to Kierkegaard's inclination to invisibility, Caputo refers to himself as a "mere scrivener," offering, as it were, nothing creative or moving on his own.

If Caputo's language of strong and weak provides a tentative non-anchored figuration for the tension he sees—or is it the tension he creates?—between reason and feeling, *logos* and *kardia*, chapter four wrestles with the play of these terms, focusing on how Caputo describes *phronesis* as "application" of an established, conventional paradigm, in which the application runs aground should the paradigm itself be called into question. But is *phronesis* mere application? Here, I urge Caputo, and others, to see rhetoric, and *phronesis*, more broadly, as a creative discourse, capable of intervening in conventional discourse and inventing new proposals. Just as Caputo offers his new proposal of weak theology that plays parasitically off variations of strong theology, which Caputo believes is a dying paradigm, so, *phronesis* might fit more harmoniously with Caputo's language of *metanoetics* than he allows.

Chapter Five picks up the notion of "invitational rhetoric" to explore and explain how Caputo's non-authoritative model of *theopoetics* opens onto the work of political and cultural transformation or the *doing* of action. Here, I will show how Caputo's rich language of "call and response" offers a poetic/rhetorical reformulation of the more traditional theological language of *revelation* and *faith*[16], focusing now not on right belief but on the response of public action, or *theopraxis*.

Chapters one through five provide something of a rhetorical prolegomenon to the work of chapter six, in which I discuss how the names of the classical topics of Christian theology—e.g., creation of humanity in the "Image of God;" sin, as the turning away from that good image; Christology, as the healing of that turning away and renewal of the image, etc.—provide not so much a fixed structure for the continuing work of theology, but an interactive and open space, focusing, in particular, on Caputo's rhetorical/*theopoetic* shaping of these topics in service of his proposal for a weak theology. As with Caputo's understanding of the name of God, that it is not the *name, but what is going on in the name* that matters, so also for the intersecting topics of "Image of God," "sin," "Christ," etc.: it is not the name of the topic, but what is going on in that name that matters. And what matters yet more is how these *interconnected* moves establish a visionary, *luring*, proposal that seeks the renewal of the world.

16. Hereafter, revelation and faith.

While Caputo is unfamiliar with rhetorical scholar, Davis, I find her engagement of Emmanuel Lévinas, in chapter seven, exploring the distinctiveness of rhetoric *vis a vis* hermeneutics to be suggestive of a shareable, if shifting, ground between herself and Caputo. And, in my conclusion, I turn to Caputo's request that we consider *The Weakness of God* to be his *Confessions*, which I take to be his active acknowledgment of being shaped by key voices of Christian tradition, even as he breaks with their interpretation of reality, and ventures into a space of profound difference—still seeking, however, what it means for us to listen, to speak, and to act on what Jesus called "The Empire of God."[17]

---

17. In translating the Greek term *basilea* as "Empire" I am following the Westar Institute's *Scholars Version*.

I

Can I Get an Amen?

THE PRIORITY OF AUDIENCE IN RHETORIC AND WEAK THEOLOGY

"Who wants a weak God?" theologian Catherine Keller asks rhetorically in her review of Caputo's *The Weakness of God*. As she writes with some humor:

> Feminist theology can hardly embrace a weak theology for ourselves (though we might not mind it if you guys do it). In order to grow our public strength we have followed the call and the image of an alternative power, a power that does not lord it over, a power of empowerment.[1]

Keller names the question everyone, including Caputo, is thinking: "Who, in their right mind wants a weak God?" And, in this passage, she shifts the question from being one about God to being one about the particular audience in which she is invested. Consider her phrase "in order to grow our public strength." With that language, she calls attention not to a logical or poetic motive, but a strategic one. Precisely because feminist theology seeks to engage inequalities within political, cultural, and theological discourse, Keller does not feel she can forgo the question of social power. Her response is as illuminating as it is hilarious. "We might not mind if you guys do it." A response that calls attention to how audiences—by gender, race, social location, and status—have differing agendas and strategies. It is as if she is in an

---

1. Keller, Review of *Weakness of God*, 137.

editorial meeting with Caputo, asking, "What's the audience for this idea? Who wants a weak God?" There has got to be a twist. Even as Caputo praises the creativity, vitality, and forcefulness of Keller's work as a key example of what he calls for under the name of *theopoetics*, he has already been at work developing that twist.

In the opening chapter of Paul's First Letter to the Corinthians, Caputo locates a foothold for his utterly foolish proposal, namely Paul's reversal of wisdom and foolishness. From the NRSV, beginning at verse 27:

> God chose what is foolish in the world to shame the wise; God chose what is weak in the world to shame the strong.[28]God chose what is low and despised in the world, things that are not, to reduce to nothing things that are, so that no one might boast in the presence of God.[30]

In *Weakness*, Caputo writes that this passage is "key to what is called the kingdom in the Synoptics."

> God chose the 'outsiders,' the people deprived of power, wealth, education, high birth, high culture. Theirs is a 'royalty' of outcasts . . . the word kingdom is being used ironically . . . to refer to . . . the very people who are precisely the victims of the world's power.[2]

In that first chapter, Paul knows that he must either recast and transform the culturally assumed Roman understanding of the cross as a symbol of criminality, torture, and humiliation or face the cultural reality that his proclamation will be as dead as Jesus on that Roman cross. As one reads Paul's words, one can overhear him wrestling with the question, "Who wants a crucified savior?" It is the impossibility of the rhetorical situation that haunts both Paul's and Caputo's language. No one wants a crucified savior, or, which is to say the same thing, a weak God. Not even a weakling.

In Paul's response that "the foolishness of God is greater than the wisdom of men (sic), that "wisdom is perfected in weakness," and "we preach the foolishness of Christ crucified," one might hear a yet more ancient take on that rhetorical turn, namely Socrates' or Plato's awareness that appearances can be misleading and that people who appear wise might be foolish, and *vice versa*.

Paul's first chapter provides a rhetorical foothold for Caputo's wider strategy of cultural reversal. What if, Caputo seems to ask, in this twenty-first century age of empire, a weak theology is exactly what is needed? When pressed by one interviewer about the meaning of "weakness" in his work,

---

2. Caputo, *Weakness of God*, 46.

Caputo responded that his use of "weakness" was "a polemical one."³ Just to be sure I checked in with an online dictionary.

> Polemic is contentious rhetoric intended to support a specific position by forthright claims and to undermine the opposing position. A person who writes polemics, or speaks polemically, is called a polemicist. Polemic can also refer to a piece of writing or a speech in which a person strongly attacks or defends a particular opinion, person, idea, or set of beliefs. The word traces back to Greek *polemikos,* which means "warlike" or "hostile" and in turn comes from the Greek noun *polemos,* meaning "war."⁴

Quite a set of definitions for a "weak theology." Yet, from a rhetorical perspective, Don Compier agrees with Caputo's response. "Rhetoric," he insists, "is polemical, or what [Kenneth] Burke calls 'agonistic.'" Compier continues:

> Cicero frequently compares the training of the orator with that of the gladiator . . . The emphasis on the stirring of passion adds to the inherently combative tenor of the persuasive profession. Philosophers may enjoy the luxury of quiet retreat in the search of truth, but Cicero warmly affirms that it is the part of the wise man [sic] to concern himself with public affairs, with all their clamor and divisiveness.⁵

Caputo, I submit, is a polemicist, engaging in "contentious argument intended to support a specific position."⁶ In the following passage, Caputo combines humor, irony, and hyperbole to mock Christianity's history of doctrinal power.

> The discourse of God is a discourse on the master words par excellence, the Lord of history, and the master of the universe, the royal power omnipotent. Is God not the dream of power aplenty, of omnitude and plentitude and plenopotentiarity, of exnihilaotry and annihilatory power, 'of being as presence, as Parousia, as life without *différance*'? . . . Can one imagine a

---

3. See Dooley, "From Radical Hermeneutics," 217. Caputo may also have Kierkegaard in mind here. In *How to Read Kierkegaard*, Caputo notes: "One quality that remained of the earlier Kierkegaard was the laughter . . . The liveliness of the polemics—he was polemical by nature, he said—[it] revived his sagging spirits." 119.

4. See: What is the definition of "polemical"—Search (bing.com), November 28, 2023

5. Compier, *What is Rhetorical Theology?* 11. Even as I write this a review of Jack Caputo's latest book *What to Believe?*, has the subtitle, "Caputo throws down the gauntlet."

6. Caputo, *Radical Hermeneutics,* 217.

> more permanent presence or a more prestigious *ousia* or a more powerful *parousia* than the 'God' under whose protection the religious powers that be huddle for protection?⁷

And if one did not catch Caputo's ironic, sarcastic, digs at the classical tradition in that paragraph, the very next one sharpens the bite.

> Can one imagine any more sovereign power than God's? Can one imagine anything more supportive of the established order, anything more top-down, more entrenched in the status quo, anything more immobilized, actualized, contented, and *nunc stans* (eternity in a single moment) than religion and religion's "God?" . . . Is not the very idea of God as the sovereign lord of the universe the very model after which every terrestrial sovereignty is designed?⁸

In these two, clearly rhetorical paragraphs, one can see Caputo laying out the organizing dichotomy of the work, aligning strong theology with assertions of omnipotence and sovereignty, with hierarchy, with the directional imagery of 'up,' with metaphysical certainty, with permanence, with the immobility of *presence*, with conventionality, and the status quo, and weak theology with uncertainty all the way down.

In his essay, "The Weight of Rhetoric: Studies in Cultural Delirium," Thomas Farrell asks the question: "Why is magnitude, and its endlessly fascinating ambiguities, an apt subject for rhetoric?" The etymology of the word comes from the Latin meaning "great of size or extent."⁹ "Greatness" moves easily to the language of strength and power. Responding to his question, Farrell moves quickly beyond the notion of magnitude as an issue of literal size.

> Magnitude—in its myriad of manifestations—seems essential to the most important concerns of traditional rhetoric: namely, whether an audience may care about any topic sufficiently to attend to it, to engage it, and to act upon it.¹⁰

In other words, "magnitude," in rhetorical terms, is a question of mattering, of how things come to matter or fail to. Does anybody care? Farrell's description fits well with a central anxiety running throughout Caputo's *Weakness*,

---

7. Caputo, *Weakness of God*, 32.
8. Caputo, *Weakness of God*, 32.
9. Ed. Mish, et al, *Merriam Webster's Collegiate Dictionary*, 748.
10. Farrell, "Weight of Rhetoric," 162.

and other works, namely, whether his weak theology has a "prayer's chance" of being taken seriously. What if no one cares? . . . But maybe . . . What if?

What if traditional claims of a strong all-powerful God, are not only out of joint with the times but also injurious to the extent they encourage a divinely authorized imperialism that has proven responsible for vast, global swaths of slavery, slaughter, poverty, disease, and destruction of religions and cultures? Farrell writes: "despite its traditional and quite justifiable association with the preservation of cultural truism, [rhetoric] may also perform an act of critical interruption, where the taken for granted practices of a culture are concerned."[11] He continues:

> The phenomenon of rhetorical interruption juxtaposes the assumptions, norms, and practices of a people so as to prompt a reappraisal of where they are culturally, what they are doing, and where they are going.[12]

This interruptive character of rhetoric can be understood as a more prophetic, deconstructive critique, in line with Caputo's call for a weak theology over against strong theology's arrogance.

In seeking to challenge and change the operative strong system of Christianity, with its criteria of right belief in the omnipotent God of tradition, Caputo challenges the assumptions of what matters in the work of theology, not by using what he calls "hard arguments" as found in metaphysics and the institutional powers of infallibility, dogma, and fundamentalist assertions, but by using figurative, indirect, images clustered around weakness, around the parables of Jesus, and the impossible kingdom of a weak God. Yet, the partial—and yes, I mean "partial" in both senses of the word—stance that he takes is, as we pointed out in his discussion of Paul on the "foolishness of the cross," a reaching for the grand style of rhetoric.

Even as he describes himself at points as a "mere scrivener," minimizing the role of any rhetorical gifts he might possess, his words speak evocatively and forcefully to an age, a culture, in profound transition. He does so not with a logical, know-it-all solution but by luring us out of ourselves with the possibility of a call, from we know not where, but which, if answered will turn our lives upside down if we have any luck at all.

---

11. Farrell, *Norms of Rhetorical Culture*, 258.
12. Farrell, *Norms of Rhetorical Culture*, 258.

SUPPOSE A SHIFT FROM STRONG TO WEAK

In *Metaphors We Live By*, George Lakoff and Mark Johnson argue for a set of metaphorical moves that are basic to us as embodied creatures. All things being equal, they explain, "up" is better than "down," "forward" is better than "backward," "strong" is better than "weak."

In *Rhetoric and Human Consciousness: A History*, Craig R. Smith takes up Kenneth Burke's notion of "image-clusters" to analyze one of Ronald Reagan's most famous speeches, his 1964 address on behalf of Barry Goldwater called "A Choice, Not an Echo." Smith opens his analysis by asking:

> What is the dichotomy established by the imagery in this discourse? Reagan gives us a 'cue' when he says, 'There is only an up or down,' referring to the pathway of government policy. He identifies 'up' with 'us,' 'we,' and 'individualism' throughout the speech; he equates 'down' with 'them,' 'they,' and 'totalitarianism.' By paragraph 19 of the speech, Reagan has identified 'private enterprise' with 'up' and 'big government' with 'down.' He fills out the dialectic clusters by envisioning private funds as 'protecting' while Social Security is pictured as 'a bare cupboard.'[13]

Reagan plays to the conventional wisdom, that 'up' is better than 'down,'" to identify who is "in" and who is "out," who's higher and who's lower on the mattering map—aligning private enterprise with "good" and "big government" with "evil"—thus creating image-clusters that do his arguing for him. Reagan doesn't have to argue on behalf of these alignments, he simply invokes them as common-sense entailments, positing them, with the insider confidence that "this is how it really is." Caputo's organizing trope of weak theology, by contrast, symbolically refuses to identify with the imagistic conventions of power. It does just the opposite.

Here, I have set side-by-side the set of images and markers that Caputo aligns with strong theology" on the one hand and "weak theology" on the other. Note the growing associations and links within each list.

Strong Theology	**Weak Theology**
—metaphysics/rhetoric	—hermeneutics
—head	—heart
—*nous*	—*kardia*
—revelation as divine knowledge	—revelation as event of call
—official power/authority	—the "force" of persuasion

---

13. Smith, *Rhetoric and Human Consciousness*, 322–23.

Strong Theology	Weak Theology
—asserting the Truth of "God"	—interpreting the "Kingdom of God"
—Law	—Justice
—grounding ontology/Presence	—play of discourse
—empire	—democracy
—dogmas and declarations	—narrative, poetic language
—Theo-logic	—Theo-poetics
—conventional	—radical
—official boundaries	—open boundaries
—priority of Self	—priority of Other
—priority of insiders	—priority of those marginalized
—sovereignty	—sacred anarchy
—expert	—"seducer"
—pride	—humility
—"method"	—"coping with flux," "wiring-up"
—heavyweight	—airy, "lightweight"
—Objective reality/ physical sciences	—Subjective reality/literature
—"hard arguments"	—figurative images/prayers/tears
—invulnerable	—vulnerable
—command	—call/whisper
—demanding	—luring
—protected by absolute Truth	—courageous risk in "becoming true"
—authority to "speak"	—capacity to "listen"
—assertive	—attentive
—focus on Author/authority	—focus on Response of Reader
—"active"	—"passive"/ responsive
—authorizing violence	—call to non-violence
—invulnerability	—vulnerability
—insists on obedience	—invites response
—foundational/certainty	—nonfoundational/uncertainty
—literal	—figurative
—fixed truth	—imagination
—"realism" vs "idealism"	—"hyper-realism"

The life-worlds that Caputo invokes through these two sets of terms help make his point that "theo-logic" is really "theo-poetics." There is no syllogism holding these positions of "strong" and "weak" theology in place. Instead, with the layering of these "poetic clusters," Caputo effectively argues that there is no metaphysical reality to "strong" theology any more than there is to "weak" theology.¹⁴ The tension in these terms is itself a construction of appearances. I am influenced here by Farrell's treatment of appearances in Aristotle's *Rhetoric*. I quote at some length.

> Consider . . . this rather typical passage on honour from the beginning of Aristotle's Rhetoric. "Honour is the token of a man's (sic) being famous for doing good; but also to the man who can do good in the future. Doing good refers either to the preservation of life, or to wealth, or to some other of the good things which it is hard to get either always or at that particular place and time—for many gain honour for things which seem small, but the place and occasion account for it. The constituents of honour are: sacrifices; commemoration, in verse or prose; privileges; grants of land; front seats at civic celebrations; state burial; statues; public maintenance; among foreigners, obeisances and giving place; and such presents as are among various bodies of men regarded as marks of honour."¹⁵

Farrell comments on the passage: "For those who are less sympathetic to classical rhetoric, this sort of passage may confirm their worst stereotypes." Farrell goes on, however, pointing out that the passage seems to be a "list," concluding: "Here we have tokens and marks of honour . . . what is taken as signifying honour." He continues, "for this is an overview of the appearances of honour presented as materials for rhetoric—how honour may be recognized, presented, framed and depicted."¹⁶ And, that is what we see in the two columns of terms associated on the one hand with strong theology and on the other with weak theology. As with tokens of honor, once one has the core, signifying vocabulary that guides an ongoing discussion, one doesn't need long arguments or debates. Caputo is quite adept at identifying those tokens of weak honor and weak force by contrasting them with the more traditional and assumed marks of divine power.

In his 1996 book, *Moral Politics*, Lakoff invoked the language of metaphorical analysis to understand the then-emerging polemical discourse of Republicans and Democrats. Beginning with his analysis of the 1994 mid-term elections, in which Republicans swept the House of Representatives and installed Newt Gingerich as Speaker, Lakoff noticed that "deeply embedded in conservative and liberal politics are different models of the family. Conservatism . . . is based on a Strict Father model, while liberalism

---

14. See Jacques Derrida, "White Mythology," 223–24.

15. Farrell, *Norms of Rhetorical Culture*, 29., See also Aristotle's *Rhetoric*, [1361a25–40].

16. Farrell, *Norms of Rhetorical Culture*, 29.

is centered around a Nurturant Parent model. These two models of the family give rise to different moral systems and different discourse forms, that is, different choices of words and different modes of reasoning."[17]

Once one sees Caputo's open set of oppositional terms, as listed above, the comparison with Lakoff's project is interesting if not compelling. Caputo uses a frame similar to Lakoff's Strong Father and Nurturant Parent, namely, of a *strong*, conventional, omnipotent model of God, and a *weak* model of "God." The latter functions to interrupt conventional, strong stances, opening them to claims and appeals of justice. While Lakoff focuses on how those two models of the family generate "different moral systems," Caputo shows how the different language clusters that gather around the language of strong and weak models of God, also give rise to different theological and moral worldviews. Lakoff's analysis of metaphorical coherence dovetails with Caputo's shift to the language of *theopoetics*. If Lakoff writes explicitly to help America's political liberals compete with conservatives rhetorically, Caputo writes to encourage a theological movement, dreaming of "theologians to-come," inspired by a postmodern affirmation of breaking open the conventions of religious and cultural power that opens a new realism focused on the gift and goodness of life.

The skill that conservatives have wielded deploying this key *family* metaphor, Lakoff argues, has enabled them "not only to gain political victories but to use politics in the service of a much larger moral agenda," which, he adds, "if carried out would, ... destroy much of the moral progress made in the twentieth century."[18] Caputo, for his part, frequently underscores the profound moral and theological dilemma in continuing to celebrate "God's[19]" omnipotent power.

In Caputo's more philosophical language, his phenomenological understanding of the experiential call to *metanoia*, to transformation, finds itself doubled, enacted on the page. His notion of *metanoia*, and its related *metanoetics*, is an exercise in the "turnability" of language As he invites or calls his readers to imagine the possibility of shifting their presumptions, their paradigms of faithfulness from *belief* to *action*, he enables the reader to imagine that shift in their life by performing, as it were, or *moving*, from an image cluster gathered around omnipotent power to an image cluster gathered around weakness. "Move from *head* to *heart*, from *certainty* to *risk*,

17. Lakoff, *Moral Politics*, 12.
18. Lakoff, *Moral Politics*, 18.
19. For his part, Caputo virtually always places the word God in quotation marks, such as "God" to remind himself an others that this name "God" is a construction not a real object. For my part, I will use—when not in conversation with Caputo—the regular spelling, God.

from *facts* to *interpretation*," Caputo coaxes his reader. "Leave *the world*, and all the theological words that cling to *the world's* continued longing for certainty and power."[20] He urges them, us, through the imagery of weak theology, to live into the language of faith understood as ongoing transformation, as a movement from the idolatry of power to the faithfulness of vulnerability and hospitality. The "turnability" of language moving beyond practical or ontological reason enables a new, open play of possibilities. Hence my title: being moved by moving words.

In his more recent, *Specters of God: An Anatomy of the Apophatic Imagination* (2022), Caputo describes weak and strong theologies. First, describing *theopoetics* as weak theology, he writes:

> *Theopoetics*, which I like to call 'weak theology,' is a poetics, a loose coalition of discursive resources—paradoxes and parables, metaphors and metonyms; striking sayings and memorable stories; songs and prayers; homilies and letters; figures and images; semantic detours, deflections, and indirections; and hyperboles and ellipses—all of which collectively, seek to evoke the force of what is going on in the name (of) 'God.'[21]

In polarizing contrast to weak theology's figurative poetics, Caputo writes that strong theology "is a logic, a coherent body of concepts, propositions, and arguments that serve to clarify so far as possible, a supernatural revelation considered in principle mysterious and beyond the reach of natural reason."[22]

Significantly for our purposes, it is important to see that Caputo places rhetoric and argumentation within the parameters of strong theologies even though rhetoric, as a discipline discussed by Aristotle, deals with public issues that are inherently uncertain.

Caputo's use of these terms, "strong" and "weak," to construct a figurative and political (not metaphysical), tension between these two worldviews is Caputo's rhetorical invention. Why rhetorical? By his interactive layering of these terms, within the metaphorical play of "strong theology" and "weak theology," Caputo calls upon us, his readers, in the words of Compier, to "loosen our allegiance" to the interests of our culturally embedded strong theologies. And, in that loosening of our allegiance, he seeks from us, as well, an open-hearted embrace of his proposed weak theology

---

20. Caputo, *Weakness*, 37.
21. Caputo, *Specters*, 17.
22. Caputo, *Specters*, 17.

and its *Lebensraum*,²³ as he calls it—a life-space calling us to the work of transformation.²⁴

Caputo's oppositional lists of terms are not simply a fixed, static set. Rather, Caputo creates a dynamic, interactive motion both within each set of terms, building on one another and between each set of terms. The term "weak" theology for example, draws its provisional meaning from its rejection of "strong" theology, which assumes the reigning presence of an all-powerful deity, proclaimed in confessional theologies with a variety of absolutist claims from biblical inerrancy, to "infallible decrees," and claims to either "pure reason or supernatural revelation."²⁵

A parasitical relation, and not merely an oppositional one, exists between the two lists. Caputo's weak proposal draws its persuasive strength and rhetorical force from his critique of the conventions of strong theology. Similarly, Caputo's affirmation of "uncertainty," a term, which, again, at first, sounds negative—after all, "who wants to be uncertain?"—begins to make sense as Caputo's questions take hold.

"Suppose," Caputo luringly invites: "what if," "perhaps" those allegedly strong, solid-sounding words or phrases are no longer certain at all, no longer culturally, philosophically persuasive? What if the brokenness of the world we are living in calls us to shift our perspective, to experiment with a new possibility, to lean into the possibility of perhaps? What if, in his language of "perhaps" and "suppose," Caputo is not only proposing but also performing, enacting a new rationality? Caputo's critique of strong theology enables him to invite, to lure, his audience to consider weakness in a new light? In these moves and more, Caputo draws out and reopens Paul's risk to celebrate the foolishness of the cross.

REFUTATIVE ENTHYMEME OR A CALL FOR JUSTICE

As Caputo's Weak Theology *interrupts* traditional and modern strong theologies, inviting us readers to shift our perspective and commitments towards identifying with those on the margins of our culture, he engages

---

23. See Compier, *What is Rhetorical Theology?* 70. "And if we assume that the heart of a critical discourse is a thorough analysis of a regime to loosen allegiance to it, it does not seem farfetched to postulate that the prophetic tradition of Christian hamartiology and contemporary emancipatory intellectual praxis share a common spirit."

24. www.thoughtco.com/lebensraum-eastern-expansion-4081248 Because the Nazis used the need for *Lebensraum* (living space) as justification for their invasion of Russia, their image comes with a good bit of moral ambiguity.

25. Caputo, *Weakness of God*, 119.

what Farrell calls a "refutative enthymeme." In his work, *Norms of Rhetorical Culture*, Farrell spells out what he means by this term through an analysis of Jesse Jackson's 1988 Democratic Convention Address, in which Jackson described the "moral challenge of our day," in terms of "economic violence." Within that "mainstream audience of convention delegates," Jackson's words call them and the wider, viewing audience to identify with those at the margin who are genuinely struggling.[26]

> They work hard everyday . . . they catch the early bus. They work every day. They raise other people's children. They work everyday. They clean the streets. They work everyday. They drive dangerous cabs. They work everyday. They change the beds you slept in in these hotels last night and can't get a union contract. They work everyday.
>
> No, no, they are not lazy! Someone must defend them because it's right, and they cannot speak for themselves. They work in hospitals. I know they do. They wipe the bodies of those who are sick with fever and pain. They empty their bedpans. They clean out their commodes. No job is beneath them, and yet when they get sick they cannot lie in the bed they made up every day. America, that is not right.[27]

As he witnesses to their menial labor, their exhaustion, and their lack of upward mobility, Jackson challenges a key cultural myth of the American "middle class." "What is being refuted, asks Farrell?

> The reprocessed Social Darwinist dream of late capitalist America. Recall Herbert Spencer's version of the enthymeme. All premises stated, it scanned thus: Free enterprise encourages hard work. Hard work leads to success. Success = Justice. Usually, all the premises are not stated, of course. As in most unexamined dogma, they do not need to be stated. This is the theme of the Protestant ethic, of every Horatio Alger novel, and of most Hollywood history. And lest we forget, it was the theme of Ronald Reagan's "Morning in America mythology . . . This is what Jackson set out to refute.[28]

But "how," Farrell asks, "does that refutation work?"

---

26. Farrell, *Norms of Rhetorical Culture*, 258.
27. Farrell, *Norms of Rhetorical Culture*, 258–59.
28. Farrell, *Norms of Rhetorical Culture*, 258–59.

First, by presenting a rarely examined world of counter-appearances. Not only does the repetition counter the myth that the poor are lazy and don't want to work; it is punctuated by a recurring arrested temporal development—that still they they are poor and, most memorably that they are denied satisfaction of the minimal, menial needs they minister to in others. How is this validated? Through the audience's own verbalized assent . . . and second by presenting these menial, usually invisible acts of servitude within a public forum and linking them to the agent as victim . . . This is the first political campaign in many years that has spoken from outside the margins of the political culture without ever abandoning the voice and strategy of direct address.[29]

I have quoted from Farrell at length because Caputo's call for a shift to weak theology, refuting the myth of Christian certainty and Christian superiority, is similar to Jackson's effort. Just as Jackson's intonation of "they work hard every day" plays parasitically off the enthymeme assumed in the American myth of hard work leading inevitably to success, so Caputo's articulation of weak theology plays off the near-ubiquitous premise that unyielding belief in God's providential power leads to worldly success, access to power, and eternal salvation. If Jackson identifies the real problem, the "moral challenge" of the day as "economic violence," Caputo focuses on the threat of violence implied in Christian traditions of certainty and dogmatic truth.

Farrell writes that a refutative enthymeme animates "appearances from the margins of society."[30] Those appearances, in Jackson's speech, are appeals not to logic, not to the head, as it were, but far more dramatically, to the heart. Jackson wants to convey the suffering caused by this stifling economy that keeps pressing people down. And Caputo seeks to surface something of this in his attention to weakness. Does our faith move us to identify with those at the margin? Does it move us to act? Caputo's challenging appearances are not professional arguments over doctrine, but the haunting, disturbing call of Jesus' parables that invites his listeners then, but also now, to come upon a man in a ditch, or a stranger at our door, knocking at midnight. Through these appearances and numerous others, Caputo shows how Jesus' words interrupt our cultural conventions of who is in and who is out, calling out the need for us to turn from a safety-first *theo-logic* towards a prophetic *theo-poetics* that risks turning the tables on the standard conventions of Christian theology. Or, as Farrell might say, "refuting" them.

---

29. Farrell, *Norms of Rhetorical Culture*, 259–60.
30. Farrell, *Norms of Rhetorical Culture*, 259.

The case of Rosa Parks can help us grasp the meaning of Farrell's *refutative enthymeme* more clearly. At issue in her courageous stand against the culture of racism was no academic point of intellectual certainty. Her gesture, which was not a speech, but a simple public act—not the fruit of disciplined, objective research, but of courage that risked suffering the consequences of breaking the law. Parks was not trying to be neutral, but was decidedly partial; she was, likely, exhausted from work, the very image, of Jackson's portrayal of those "taking the early bus."

There is a story of Parks, who in preparation for the Montgomery Bus Boycott, attended a workshop at the Highlander Folk School's Research and Education Center, entitled "Racial Desegregation: Implementing the Supreme Court Decision," led in part by the founder of Highlander, Myles Horton.[31] According to Horton, Rosa was the "quietest participant in the workshop." Adding, "If you judge by the conventional standards, she would have been the least promising, probably."[32] That is, "least promising" for actually doing something for the cause when she returned to Montgomery. Those who spoke with her at that workshop remembered her saying that "Montgomery was the cradle of the Confederacy," and that "nothing would happen [in Montgomery] because blacks wouldn't stick together."[33] Transformation, genuine change, seemed *impossible*.[34] But then, five months later, back in Montgomery, she acted, and the *impossible* happened. A simple act of refusal. An act that broke the law in the name of justice. Another *refutative enthymeme*. This one refutes the white myth that some are more equal—more deserving of respect and deference—than others.

Could Parks's act have remained invisible? Yes. As a moment, as an *event* in the broader *event* of the Montgomery Bus Boycott, however, her act of courage became the image, the face, the key *appearance*, in Farrell's vocabulary, that sealed the argument of the protestors. Not a logical argument,

---

31. See: Jeanne Theoharis, "Rosa Parks's Transformative Two Weeks at the Highlander Research and Education Center" at: Rosa Parks's Transformative Two Weeks at the Highlander Research and Education Center—Beacon Broadside: A Project of Beacon Press.

32. Theoharis, "Rosa Park's Transformative Two Weeks."

33. Theoharis, "Rosa Park's Transformative Two Weeks.

34. Caputo, *What Would Jesus Deconstruct?*, 78–79. Caputo, following Derrida, understands "the Impossible," as a term of hope. Placing it within the notion of "deconstruction," he writes: "Deconstruction is affirmation of the impossible, of the coming of the event." A deconstruction turns the language of despair into a language of hope, of a call for transformation that we cannot see coming. "Deconstruction is not realism because it is in love with illusion, but because it desires what is more than the real rather than settling for what is less, for the real is always deconstructible."

but a figurative one, a poetic, and rhetorical one. And it is this kind of transformation that Caputo longs for in his readers.

As skilled as his argument is in skewering theology's focus on logic and certainty—Caputo does not own—as Gaonker points out—that his discourse is rhetorical, not even recognizing the rhetorical character of Jesus' preaching in the context of the Roman Empire, much less noticing the rhetorical character of his *theopoetic* proposal. And so, as Biesecker points out, the rhetorical character of the work tends to be avoided or silenced in Caputo's desire to disappear into the appeal of the work. Yet, here again, he is not alone but in the company of other courageous figures seeking to open a closed culture.

In his numerous works, Caputo frequently refers to the political speeches of several figures, including Dr. Martin Luther King, Jr., Bobby Kennedy, Abraham Lincoln, and Franklin Delano Roosevelt—tacitly acknowledging the persuasive forcefulness of their oratory in calling the nation to both account and renewal. In their voices, Caputo hears a call that moves us, the American audience, to participate, with those speakers, in calling the nation to turn from hard-heartedness towards compassion and justice. But, at no time in any of their speeches did King or Kennedy, Roosevelt or Lincoln stop or interrupt their speech to spell out the rhetorical moves they were making. They were seeking to move their audiences to speak and act on behalf of those hopes and passions that too often remain unspoken. His mention of them deserves our attention, every bit as much as his invocation of Catherine Keller, Meister Eckhart, and St. Augustine. Whether from the political or the theological side, Caputo calls on both to manifest courage on behalf of those suffering.

In the chapters that follow, we will see this theme, this focal point, return.

2

Mark 3:1–6

No *Nous* is Good News

Given Caputo's forceful language, his readers can surely see that what he means by "weakness" is not merely resistance to strong theology's institutional power and dogmatic assertions of absolute truth. Rather, it is just as importantly a call, an invitation, to an ongoing process of advocacy, urging a deepening identification with those at the margins and beyond the boundaries of conventional religious and cultural belonging, a faith of active witness on behalf of justice that reverses the assumption of who is "in" and who is "out." Nowhere, is that reversal more pivotally discussed than in Caputo's reading of the Markan text "A Man with a Withered Hand" in *The Weakness of God*.[1] The story is an important one for Caputo—"one of my favorite New Testament stories"—and of central importance to the proposal he develops in *Weakness*.[2]

To place the story in some wider context, scholars believe Mark's gospel was composed after the destruction of the Temple in 70 CE, and this story's focus on the wounded man provides a lens upon the somatic damage to our bodies that results from imperial rule, causing much hardship—no healthy hand, no manual labor. In Mark's framing of this story, we see two Jewish communities at odds on the importance of Jewish observance of the Law. At the time of Mark's redaction, there were no "Christians," so it would be a mistake to read this story in terms of Christians vs Jews. It is a

---

1. Mark 3:1–6.
2. Caputo, *Weakness of God*, 128.

thoroughly Jewish encounter involving a key, rhetorical issue of identification. How does one best belong to the Jewish community?—a question that should remind us of Farrell's point that questioning the norms of a culture is an inherently rhetorical act.

On one side are the Pharisees/leaders, who in Mark's redaction are elite figures in the upper echelons of Jewish society, who wish to insist on the importance of obedience to tradition and who wish to bring their status and the power of the Law to bear against this unruly figure, Jesus, and anyone following him. On the other side, gathered around the figure/memory of Jesus, were Jewish followers of Jesus who underscored the importance of doing justice for that vulnerable and damaged man, even on the Sabbath.

Told from the perspective of the Jewish-community-following-Jesus, the story, according to New Testament scholar, Arthur Dewey, relies on a basic trope, or convention, of Jewish stories, namely, that "leaders" always get it wrong, "It's a humorous trope that points fun at those who claim to be experts in the Law."[3] Mark's creative editing, in turn, uses Jesus' miracles and teaching to refute the Pharisees/religious leaders' claim, and to insist that the Sabbath is kept holy not by doing nothing but by healing and doing the work of justice. Here is the text from Mark as translated in the NRSV.

> Again he entered the synagogue, and a man was there who had a withered hand. They watched him to see whether he would cure him on the sabbath, so they might accuse him. And he said to the man who had the withered hand, "Come forward." Then he said to them, "Is it lawful to do good or to do harm on the sabbath, to save life or to kill?"
>
> But they were silent. He looked around at them with anger; he was grieved at their hardness of heart and said to the man, "Stretch out your hand." He stretched it out, and his hand was restored. The Pharisees went out and immediately conspired with the Herodians against him, how to destroy him.

This story follows directly upon three encounters between Jesus and the Pharisees/religious leaders. Here they are together, yet again, and it appears from the narrative that they—the Pharisees or Jewish leaders—have been waiting for Jesus. They want to see if he will heal the man with a crippled hand on the Sabbath and thereby violate the Law, which insists on a day of complete rest.

In the story itself, Mark's Jesus wastes no time confronting those conventional defenders of the Law. He calls the passive, broken man forward, calling him into public view as a focal point of confrontation. Jesus then

---

3. Conversation with Dr. Arthur J. Dewey, October 2023.

asks the Pharisees a very loaded question that plays, perhaps, to the audience that has gathered. "On the Sabbath is it permitted to do good or to do evil, to save life or to kill?" And Mark adds, immediately, "But they remained silent."

Jesus' rhetorical question, his call, as it were, to the Pharisees, is direct and asks for an immediate response. He calls them "on the carpet," as Caputo might say. Instead of responding, they choose avoidance; they choose to be silent, which is Mark's tacit way of either re-stating their position that the Sabbath is kept holy by doing nothing, or, showing that in this debate they have nothing to say. Perhaps both.

Jesus, for his part, comments/acts in a way that answers his own question. Saying to the man, "Stretch out your hand." "He stretched it out and his hand was restored." In contrast to the Pharisees/leaders who had nothing to say, much less, do, Jesus' words act immediately to heal the man. What could the Pharisees say to this? They could speak only bitterly among themselves; these experts in the Law could not grasp the unconditional call to do justice.[4] And if that were not enough, it is they, in the end, who plot to kill on the Sabbath, by hatching a plot to "destroy him."

In his analysis, Caputo is aware of a complication. Acknowledging that the term "Pharisees" should be "taken with a grain of salt," he continues: "The New Testament authors were engaged in a polemic with the Jews from whom, by the end of the first century they were splitting off, and in their efforts to give the Jews a black eye, their target of choice was the Pharisees."[5] Instead of pursuing the implications of this polemic at work amidst the New Testament writings—a polemic engaged in the ambiguities of group identity in the period following the destruction of the Temple, and immersed in dynamics of power, e.g., from boundary formation to purity regulations to debates over inclusion/exclusion, and more—Caputo chooses to side-step that dynamic to focus on the theme of "hardness of heart." Without even mentioning that translation's reference to Pharoah as an enemy of God, which again suggests that Jesus is engaged in a real debate with real consequences, Caputo addresses the reader and changes the subject.

> Notice that the biblical story says that Jesus grieved over the hardness of heart of these high-ranking authorities. He did not disagree with their arguments and come back with a counter-example, or a more comprehensive covering theory. He did not think this was a dispute to be settled by the weight of "good

---

4. See chapter six, below, on Caputo's reading of Derrida's essay, "The Force of Law."
5. Caputo, *Weakness*, 139.

reasons" one way or the other. He did not think it was a matter of reason, of *logos* or *nous* at all, but of the heart,"[6]

Caputo's invitation to the reader to "notice" is a call for his readers to focus on Jesus' felt grief in response to the leaders' hardness of heart, what the Scholar's Version translates as Jesus' being "exasperated at their closedmindedness."[7] Caputo's rhetorical nudging of *us*, his readers, to focus on what Jesus "was not thinking," as it were, is an attempt to frame the pericope in terms that fit Caputo's strong and weak categories: reason, or *nous* representing strong, authoritative "Law" vs. the heart, or *kardia*, representing the weak, vocative call of justice.[8] Caputo introduces into the story his own preoccupation with Greek philosophy, with *nous*, and *logos* as the *real* problem that Jesus confronts here. There is no textual evidence, however, that either Jesus or Mark is thinking of abstract rationality at all in this passage.

At issue was the welfare and somatic well-being of those suffering the consequences of empire. Even as Caputo uses the biblical text to create a philosophical gulf between head and heart, he ignores the fact, as it were, that Mark has framed this and other healing stories, e.g., the story of the paralytic in chapter two—as debates! Indeed, Mark, as opposed to Caputo, sees a Jesus, across these four miracle stories who is far more comfortable with public debate and reasoning than Caputo seems to be. The story of "A Man with a Withered Hand," shows Mark's Jesus to be quite canny of the religious leaders' motives and keenly aware of how to box them in rhetorically, actually silencing them for fear of the public's response.[9]

Yet, even in the face of this Markan use of miracle to declare Jesus the winner of his debate with official, Jewish leaders, Caputo resists aligning debate, argument, propositions, or proposals with the stories of Jesus' healing and preaching the justice of the Empire of God. By thus situating rhetoric, argumentation, and debate within the fallen language, as it were, of strong theology, it is as if Caputo cannot acknowledge the obvious, namely that Jesus' own very creative and courageous works make an appeal, a "soft argument," if you will, that offers a proposal, structures a debate, and uses reason within and through his rich overlay of tropical, metaphorical entailments. It is difficult to see how Caputo can insist on the importance of *theopoetics*

---

6. Caputo, *Weakness of God*, 142.

7. See Miller, ed., *The Complete Gospels*, 28.

8. See chapter seven where I discuss the importance of Derrida's lecture/essay "The Force of Law" as an analog for Caputo's discussion of God.

9. In *What Would Jesus Deconstruct?*, 43, Caputo notes that "Jesus himself seems to be no small verbal master."

being political without having recourse to rhetorical engagement, which is decidedly not simply polishing a position one has already decided upon.

In contrast to the powerful weapons of strong theology, weak theology has only, says Caputo, the "whisper of the persuasiveness of what it has to say." Persuasiveness, his whispering seems to say, is a weak force. But it also might be the case, that in his whispering Caputo has been trying ever-so-silently to smuggle persuasion out of its traditional and contemporary belonging within the discipline of rhetoric and into the play of his weak theology, and in the process, smuggle in the only force he really has.[10]

In contrast to Caputo's placement of rhetoric, debate, argumentation, and proposal within the camp of strong theology, I suggest that the poetic and the rhetorical are richly entangled. Rhetoric is not simply, as Caputo seems to want it, in the rationality closet; instead, it belongs as a *"tertium quid*,"[11] in tension between strong and weak theologies, drawing not only on *nous*, but on *pathos* and *ethos*.[12] Thinking for a moment with Jacques Derrida in *White Mythology*: in moving "from philosophy to rhetoric," the linguistic turn moves into an uncertainty that neither classical nor modern philosophy can contain—the uncertainty of metaphor, which by its catachretic[13] character breaks out of old connections and breaks open new ones.[14]

My claim, again, is that Caputo need not separate so strongly the poetic from the rhetorical. I find in Caputo's weak *theopoetics* an imaginative force turning the world upside down. Such moments, such *events*, happen as rhetorical events that call readers and hearers to risk their lives to make the wisdom of Jesus' parables come true. As he notes in *Weakness*, "the call is itself constituted by being heard."[15] One speaks of a "call," only in the event of what it (whatever it was) has moved one to respond, to do. But, just here, Caputo longs to protect the purity of the call, by having it—by definition—sealed in completion, "by our heeding and not simply hearing."[16]

---

10. In contrast to the conventional all-powerful theology, an intentional commitment to non-violence rhymes with a long-held defense of the public importance of rhetoric, going back to Cicero. Namely, that public discourse is an alternative to violence as such. Insofar as weak theology, in Caputo's words, "lays down" the weaponized absolutes of strong theology "in favor of peace," it calls for rhetorical engagement.

11. See Caputo, *Hermeneutics*, 11.

12. See Caputo, *Hermeneutics*, 139–41.

13. From the Greek, *catechresis*, the term as used in contemporary rhetorical theory, points to the way the unexpected combination of terms and images that occur in metaphor or other tropes like hyperbole can break open or invent new meaning.

14. Derrida, "White Mythology," 209.

15. Caputo, *Weakness of God*, 114.

16. Caputo, *Weakness of God*, 114.

What Caputo longs for, prays and weeps for is that his words might be a vehicle by which his readers might be moved to respond, to act, to move in new and better ways. And yet, as we will see in the coming chapter, Caputo remains somewhat torn on this point. With Kierkegaard, he longs to be invisible, to be out of the way, as it were. His expressed caution to avoid any kind of "rouge theology" leads him, as we will see in chapter four, to a place where he seeks to deny the importance of rhetoric—arguing for a movement from "call" to "response" that, like here, appears automatic—moving, as it were, from our ears to our feet—with no further need of encouragement from beyond ourselves.

3

Kierkegaard and the Passions of a Scrivner

To enrich our understanding of Caputo's theopoetic proposal, and his marginalization of rhetoric, I turn to his 2008 book, *How to Read Kierkegaard*. Caputo's exploration of Kierkegaard's focus on reading and writing aligns with his *theopoetic* focus on the play of "call and response," asking his readers to risk embracing not only the existential possibility of experiencing an unconditional call upon one's life, but also the possibility of being so moved by, seduced by, or persuaded by their reading that it calls them not to believe but to act publicly, without the protection of authority.

If there is a voice or a style that Caputo "repeats forward," it is Kierkegaard's.[1] There is the biting sarcasm, the laughter at power, the sense of freedom that comes in carrying through on one's public obligation to "weigh in," as Farrell might say. Kierkegaard is, of course, one of the most passionate, biting, and subjective of Christian theologians—taking aim at the established Danish church of nineteenth-century Christendom. Writing with the critical zeal of Nietzsche, while yet holding open the passionate possibility of a leap of faith, Kierkegaard is a crucial precursor for Caputo.

Commenting on the creativity of Kierkegaard's complex authorship, including his use of pseudonymous authors, Caputo claims, with Kierkegaard, "that the most subjective truths can never be achieved by objective

---

1. See Caputo, *Hermeneutics*, 130–31, for his discussion of the terms "repeat forward" and "repeat backward."

means or be given independent objective status."² Recalling Farrell's discussion of *magnitude,* notice how Caputo's language of the "objective" over against the "subjective" plays to Caputo's comparative image clusters of strong and weak. "Objective" arguments have the "real weight" of evidence, and an obvious "gravity," connected to real power. "Subjective" claims, on the other hand, have virtually no weight at all.³ Yet, some truths, says Caputo, cannot be known by theory or universal reason:

> As St. Augustine said, there are certain things we can learn only if we love what we are seeking to learn about. The real meaning of saying 'God is love' is forged and acquired in subjective life; its real meaning is what it means in my life.⁴

Or, as Augustine writes in *Confessions,* book thirteen, "my love is my weight." (13.10) This knowing, from "passionate" response"⁵ is not "neutral" but always partial in the double sense of being both incomplete and aligning with others' interests. Indeed, in *The Weakness of God,* Caputo underscores this non-method of passionate subjectivity. The genuine religious author, says Caputo, appeals to the reader's passion, not to their certainty. As Caputo puts it: "If all theology means is to treat God as the subject matter of an objectifying discourse, then theology is not possible. For God is only given in prayer."⁶ Here Caputo aligns himself with Kierkegaard's passion:

> He wanted to address that secret inner chamber where the single individual is absolutely alone before God . . . Having set aside all the distractions and diversions that press in from the world, we close the door and confront ourselves. That is why Kierkegaard elsewhere advised reading his books alone and out loud. The ancient Augustinian formula 'before God' (*coram*

---

2. Caputo, *How to Read Kierkegaard,* 13. Caputo writes: "The truth 'for me' does not mean arbitrariness or caprice, believing anything one likes. It signifies inner resolve, where the 'for me' "means the truth that personally transforms my life."

3. To be clear, Kierkegaard didn't use the language of strong and weak; that is Caputo weaving of Kierkegaard's voice, passion, and concerns into his own proposal.

4. Caputo, *How to Read Kierkegaard,* 14.

5. Caputo, *How to Read Kierkegaard,* 13. "If Christianity is 'true' it is true in the sense that the Scriptures speak of when it is said of Jesus that he is 'the way, the truth, and the life', meaning that its truth is a way of a living in the truth If you do not have in your heart the love of your neighbor of which the New Testament speaks; if you are not loving and forgiving in your life; if you do not inscribe this love into your personal existence, then you are not 'in the truth' in the 'existential' sense." Notice, again, the way Caputo stays away from speech/language moving one towards the truth. He leaps right to action.

6. Caputo, *Weakness of God,* 285–86.

Deo) is Kierkegaard's primal scene ... He himself as a religious author is the third man (sic) out, one man (sic) too many in this primal scene, and so he must make himself as light and airy a thing as possible. By writing under a pseudonym, he was trying to be invisible.[7]

Like Augustine in the *Confessions*, Kierkegaard seeks to be both out-of-the-way of such a sacred experience *and* the medium of the religious encounter. If Kierkegaard was attempting to be invisible, precisely to be out of the reader's way for experiencing that absolute aloneness before God, so also is Caputo in his invitational rhetoric. What Caputo writes of Jacques Derrida in *What Would Jesus Deconstruct*, namely of his "love of experimental writing, of writing in such a way as to 'produce an event,'" can be said of Caputo as well.[8] Again and again, he performs an invitational dynamic on the page that enacts the possibility of an event, of a call, that, in turn, calls for a response from within the reader.[9] Continuing this line of invisibility, Caputo writes:

> One who dares to write about becoming a Christian cannot be like other writers, an authority, a heavyweight, an 'objective' author, like a world historian. He must be like a ghost, light and airy. Objective truths admit in principle of direct

---

7. Caputo, *How to Read Kierkegaard*, 76–77.
8. Caputo, *What Would Jesus Deconstruct?*, 50.

9. About the "author" and "reader" as "positions," Caputo writes: "Think of the distinction between an 'author' and a 'reader' as the difference between two different 'positions', an ideal sending position and a real receiver position. Seen thus, even Søren Aabye Kierkegaard, as a real person, is situated in the position of a reader. Kierkegaard too is a 'receiver' of these words about becoming a Christian, not an author or an authority, and as far removed from actually being a Christian as the next chap ... The 'author' is a position stationed in ideality, and his actuality is not important ... The deployment of a pseudonym simply intensifies or makes palpable something that is structurally true of any author. The real author may be considered as an empirical ... personality ... as a real or efficient cause of the books ... Or an 'author' may be considered *as such*, as a 'position' from which ideal possibilities issue, while 'we' occupy the 'readerly position', a position always stationed in 'existence.'" (74) Caputo may also have the notion of the "death of the author" in mind when he writes of himself as a mere scrivener. That language of scrivener may be influenced by Roland Barthes' use of the term. "No longer the focus of creative influence, the author is merely a 'scriptor' (a word Barthes uses expressly to disrupt the traditional continuity of power between the terms 'author' and 'authority'). The scriptor exists to produce but not to explain the work and 'is born simultaneously with the text.' The scriptor 'is in no way equipped with a being preceding or exceeding the writing, [and] is not the subject with the book as predicate.' Every work is 'eternally written here and now,' with each re-reading, because the 'origin' of meaning lies exclusively in 'language itself' and its impressions on the reader." See: https://en.wikipedia.org/wiki/The_Death_of_the_Author

communication: the logician puts the proof on the board. But subjective truths require indirection, even seduction, or ghosts that haunt us, whispering words that elicit or awaken a movement in the freedom of the reader . . .[10]

Invoking "strong" "heavyweight," and "objective" authors, Caputo continues to fill out his strong/weak image clusters.[11] The authentic religious author of weak theology seeks to be one "without authority," who seeks to get out of the way of the reader responding to the call of God. Caputo adds that "at this primordial scene, Kierkegaard himself merely assists, as an occasion, a humorist, an ironist who is here one minute and gone the next."[12]

Anyone familiar with Caputo's numerous works and appreciates Caputo's own humorous and ironic voice can now better appreciate how that "voice" is more than humorous; it is strategic, inviting the reader, as it were, "to pay no attention" to the proper name on the jack-et cover. Still, Caputo, like Derrida, longs for his writing to be a vehicle of the event of the call, to prompt an event in the reader to move away from hardness of heart and towards compassion, towards the other.

Like Kierkegaard, Caputo suggests he desperately wants to "get out of the way," perhaps beyond his own rhetorical interests. One can imagine him weeping, shedding tears, longing to be free of rhetoric, of his own voice, and its interests in book sales, and to speak a word that prompts genuine confrontation and healing.[13]

One might now better see—given his identification with, or use of Kierkegaard—why Caputo wants to avoid rhetoric, wants to avoid argument and debate; he does not want, as we noted earlier, the text to be about him and his "authority." Precisely because Caputo longs to be a vehicle, opening up that impossible space of the event for a new, potential audience, he seeks to minimize his stature and get out of the way. But in order to do that he first has to get in the way. To explain this "delicate communicative art," Caputo aligns Kierkegaard with Derrida's "paradox of the gift." "Knowing how to give a gift in such a way as not to create a feeling of dependence in

---

10. Caputo, *How to Read Kierkegaard*, 76–77.

11. See Caputo, *Radical Hermeneutics*, 214, Caputo acknowledges his longing to be a "heavyweight," as it were. "Like all authors, I want to create the illusion that I am the master of this text, that there is a certain progress in these three chapters, that they are edging toward a conclusion." In *Weakness*, he seems determined to let go of that "illusion."

12. Caputo, *How to Read Kierkegaard*, 77.

13. I remember listening to Langdon Gilkey, perhaps lecturing on Kierkegaard, in which he noted the irony of the situation facing contemporary theologians, writing of God's concern for the poor while hoping one's 401K is doing nicely.

the recipient. The task is to help readers find their own independence and freedom—without acquiring a dependence on the author."[14]

In this communicative art, however, the reader, too, is charged with an equally difficult task. "The reader, on the other hand, has the parallel task of how to read such a book, for the reader must not be merely reading a book but coming face to face with himself, before God. It is like a sermon on Sunday morning: one hears each word from the pastor as if it were coming from God and directed solely to oneself."[15] As noted above in my reference to Farrell, the reader occupies the position of "audience," (audio) receiving a call (perhaps in reading Scripture, or a novel, listening to a homily, to a political speech, etc.) and thus exposed to being moved, not only in mind but in heart, and further yet, to the work, the action of transformation.

Understood rhetorically, the reader or audience completes, (or not), the action of the author/text by being moved by it, to acting and speaking with a new, changed set of commitments, which for Caputo includes acting on behalf of those on the margins who are without voice, without power. By being open to being moved and moved to action, Caputo's "hermeneutical" reader is called upon to, in turn, become rhetorical, called upon to complete the call that calls for a response, by being moved to speak/write/act in a transformed way, by a discourse without authority save by the "whisper of the persuasiveness of what it has to say."[16]

Just as Kierkegaard does not forget that he himself is a reader, as one who is addressed by his own works,[17] neither does Caputo. He underscores the priority of the reader, of the one who is addressed. We respond, says Caputo—"in the accusative, '*me voici.*'" And it is that sense of always already being addressed, of being an interpreter, that informs Caputo's oft-repeated line that discourse is "hermeneutics all the way down."[18] Yet, insofar as Caputo longs for his *theopoetics* to be political, the receptivity of listening needs to turn to speech and action.

PERSUADED BY WHOM?

In his discussion of religious authorship, Caputo notes that Kierkegaard pays homage to the "noble rogue," Socrates—that midwife of antiquity who understood, "the highest one human being can do for another is to educate

---

14. Caputo, *How to Read Kierkegaard*, 77.
15. Caputo, *How to Read Kierkegaard*, 77.
16. See Epigraph.
17. Caputo, *How to Read Kierkegaard*, 73.
18. Caputo, *Hermeneutics*, 141.

him into freedom, help him to stand by himself, which means that the helper must make himself anonymous, invisible, nothing at all."[19]

Throughout this discussion of the invisibility of the author and the priority of the reader in responding to the call, Caputo is no longer merely describing Kierkegaard's, or Socrates' task but his own, that of turning his reading, his interpretation, of Kierkegaard into his own proposal for a weak theology that he hopes will speak to his readers. Put another way, Caputo, with his interpretation of Kierkegaard's works, seeks to articulate the risks and responsibilities involved in writing and reading a book by which a reader might be persuaded (note the passive voice) but not by the author, as such.

Caputo presses this question further in his discussion about "authors" and "readers" in his treatment of Kierkegaard's pseudonymous writings. What some interpreters of Kierkegaard's pseudonymous authors miss, says, Caputo:

> [is] the distinction between the poetic ideality of the author and the existential actuality of the reader. Authors pose to the readers, to existing persons—to everyone from Kierkegaard to us—the task of actualization, of making the leap, of converting into reality what transpires among them as pure 'poetic' ideality . . . Kierkegaard dangles before the reader a dance of possibilities, of world views, articulated by several authors [pseudonyms], into whose play he seeks to draw the reader. But it is the task of the reader to choose for oneself, to decide, to exist—which means to actualize the ideal, to convert these idealities into the currency of existence, to make the leap.[20]

Is it only Kierkegaard who "dangles before the reader a dance of possibilities . . . seeking to draw the reader in?" Does not Caputo utilize pseudonyms in *Against Ethics* and *Weakness*, to lure the reader? Again, constructing himself as one without authority, caught up in the vast play of uncertainty, Caputo cannot dictate the objective terms of his discourse as if he were a "heavyweight," writing from a sure possession of eternal truth. He begins, instead, by dangling invitations and possibilities before his readers with words like perhaps, suppose, imagine, or what if? His own words of possibility lure us, readers, to imagine the possibility of receiving a call, of experiencing an event, an occurrence, an obligation that breaks open our traditional understandings of rational discourse and the very limited cultural horizons we inhabit.

19. Caputo, *How to Read Kierkegaard*, 78.
20. Caputo, *How to Read Kierkegaard*, 73.

If one can imagine and be open to such a call—a call, Caputo says, "from we know not where"—then it might be possible for contemporary readers, as in the experience of Augustine, in Book Eight of the *Confessions*, to respond to the call to "pick up and read." A call might be experienced in any cultural context. Virtually any text—even a "weak theology" like Caputo's—could be the vehicle, the midwife of a call-event that would challenge a reader not simply to keep on reading but to put down the book and to move one's life in a new direction. Such would be the experience of being persuaded, and yet not, claims Caputo, by Kierkegaard or by Caputo, but by one's own experience of the call, of being invited, summoned, and required to respond, to make the leap of faith. Hence the sense of existential mystery around that experience, that *event*, of a call.

Caputo enacts in his reading of Kierkegaard a type of allegory, in my view, a poetic and rhetorical move, in which the "call" that one experiences through the words on a page, is "received" as a call, but not as a call from Caputo or Kierkegaard, whose words are the mere instrumentality, mere vehicle, or container, of a call that might call me out of myself. Such a call, such an event, is not about some informational content (what Emmanuel Lévinas associates with the "said" [*le dit*] of communication) but is an interruptive call—what Lévinas associates with the disruptive "saying" (*le dire*)—that invites/demands that the receiver/reader change one's life.

To the extent that Kierkegaard and Caputo locate themselves as religious authors, the task they set themselves was/is to tap into and awaken the individual subjectivity of their readers, and enable them, in response to the call, to make the leap, the decision to change their lives. "Success in this project," Caputo writes of Kierkegaard, "would consist of prodding or agitating his readers to somehow find the truth that is true for them."[21] Caputo adds: "That would be his [Kierkegaard's] task—to defend the thought that truth is not a thought but a personal task."[22] Something to do.

Even as he attempts to explore the weak force of Kierkegaard's writing and his use of pseudonymous authors, Caputo exposes his own voice as a "poet of obligation," as a scribe, a midwife, and an ironist. Insofar as truth is not some information, some certified certainty, but a singular task, a response to a call, to a way of life—from who knows where—one needs to speak in more indirect, more poetic, but also more moving terms than in the strong, generalized, detached, assumptions of modernity. Again, "objective truths admit in principle of direct communication: the logician puts the proof on the board. But subjective truths require indirection, even

21. Caputo, *How to Read Kierkegaard*, 36.
22. Caputo, *How to Read Kierkegaard*, 16.

seduction, or ghosts that haunt us, whispering words that elicit or awaken a movement in the freedom of the reader..."[23] From within his commitment to uncertainty, Caputo seeks to nudge, invite, and encourage his readers to consider risking an openness to receiving a call that would challenge, break open, and transform their lives, not in theory but in practice.[24] Of such discourse, however, is rhetoric composed.

Kierkegaard's emphasis on the theme of "inwardness" and the figure of *the Individual* alone before God—what Caputo also picks up in his use of the language of *coram Deo*—suggests a real suspicion of rhetoric, which is to say, of public discourse. Insofar as public discourse involves what Kierkegaard calls "comparative," and not ideal, standards, public life is caught up in the aesthetic—mere comparison, which is not yet owning responsibility for the ethical. Public, or, rhetorical discourse (notice that debate is intrinsically comparative) cannot be a vehicle—cannot carry the weight—of genuine religious experience.

> In connection with the human crowd (i.e. when the individual is looking to see how the other behaves . . .) it is all right to apply a comparative standard, but in case this use of the comparative standard gets so much the upper hand that the individual in his inner man applies it to himself, then the ethical is done for.[25]

The focus on the "inner man," on "inwardness" suggests a kind of bounded hiddenness that longs to keep the acids of modernity, of public debate in civil society, at arm's length. Kierkegaard's "crowd," is precisely "the sort of people who are to be had by the dozen, who are as people mostly are in their town, and resemble one another like tin soldiers in a box."[26]

Given the extent to which Kierkegaard has influenced Caputo's discussion of reading, writing, and interpretation, it cannot be too far off to ask to what extent Kierkegaard, and perhaps Karl Barth, have informed Caputo's suspicion of rhetoric, as a kind of "rouge-like" discourse, polishing the apple of liberal theology? To the extent that Kierkegaard's view of the crowd informs Caputo's attempt to place argumentation, debate, and rhetoric over against the more genuine language of the heart, *kardia*, Caputo may want

---

23. Caputo, *How to Read Kierkegaard*, 77.

24. As Caputo writes in *Weakness of God*, "My hypothesis is that making the truth happen, *doing* hospitality, is what *constitutes* membership in the kingdom . . . That is how, according to the mad hatter's logic of the kingdom, it is precisely the *outsiders* who are *in*, while those who complacently take their membership for granted, who take their invitations to the banquet for granted, find themselves left *out*. (268–69)

25. Kierkegard, *Concluding Unscientific Postscript*, 486.

26. Kierkegard, *Concluding Unscientific Postscript*, 489.

to explore the tension between how *he* moves from Kierkegaard's suspicion of comparative thinking to his own *comparative* play of strong and weak theologies. Alongside that change, we will also see Caputo seek to shift from Kierkegaard's emphasis on "inwardness," and the category of "the Individual" to Lévinas' emphasis on the priority of the Other, which opens a door to a more complex political turn toward justice.[27]

To pull his argument off, Caputo encourages his readers to see Kierkegaard not merely as a modern thinker, but as one who, like Caputo himself, wrestled to free theology from its rationalistic, universalistic assumptions. "His [Kierkegaard's] is a kind of revolutionary anti-philosophy that turns philosophy's head in the opposite direction, toward the lowest and least and last among us—the subjective, the personal, the existential, the singular, the little 'fragments', as Climacus put it, that Hegel's vast 'system of philosophy' omits."[28]

In these lines, one can hear Caputo creatively invoking additional tropes of magnitude, namely, key themes of reversal, e.g., "little fragments," along with the "lowest," and "least" of the marginalized, to weave together a more *public* audience than Kierkegaard would have approved.

---

27. As I noted in *A Scandalous Jesus*, 147, it was theologian J. B. Metz who argued persuasively that his mentor, Karl Rahner, whose deeply existential theology, informed by Heidegger, and that shaped much of the work of the Second Vatican Council, had led theology to become too "private and individualistic. It fails," he said, "to bring into sufficient prominence the social and political dimensions of the believer's faith and responsibility."

28. Caputo, *How to Read Kierkegaard*, 17.

4

Nous, Kardia, Phronesis, Oh, My!

IN HIS BOOK, *RADICAL Hermeneutics*, Caputo suggests that his close interlocutor, Jacques Derrida had, what I would call, a rhetorical sensibility about the debates over cultural dynamics of stability and change. I quote here at length.

> I take it from Derrida that there is a kind of unresolved dialectic, a rhythmic alteration, between tentative schemes and their disruption . . . [W]hile Derrida provides no criteria for what makes for better or worse fictions, he does describe the conditions under which decisions should be reached. He thinks that things get worked out in a way which is very much like what [Richard] Rorty . . . calls the conversation of mankind (sic)—[namely,] by a kind of ongoing debate in which the forces of rhetoric clash and settle into a consensus of whose contingency it is the role of the Socratics and Derrideans to remind us, to the point of distraction and infuriation . . . Courses are decided by the most appealing insights available, the most persuasive arguments, sometimes by those who have experience and sometimes by those who have new ideas, sometimes well and sometimes disastrously. That is always how it has been.[1]

He continues:

> The upshot of Derrida's critical praxis is not confusion and anarchy, as is often claimed, but free and open debate. A good deal

---

1. Caputo, *Radical Hermeneutics*, 196.

of Derrida's goal is to make the debate fair by exposing the dismissive and exclusionary gestures that tend to characterize the ruling discourse. Students, women, blacks, gays, the retarded, minorities of all sorts, "amateurs" (= lovers, nonprofessionals, nonexperts), Jews, Catholics, atheists, scientists—all have in various ways and at various times been simply deprived of participation in 'normalized' discourse. Debate is conceived in advance to be possible only among those who conform to the ruling paradigm.[2]

In these final lines, Caputo presses on the issue of access to participation in cultural and political life. Question: When is open debate not really open? Answer: When participation is confined to those who "conform to the ruling paradigm." For Caputo, this language of "ruling paradigm" is evident in the variations of strong theology, where doctrinal certainty functions to limit who can speak and who cannot.

It is weak theology that presses for open debate, that longs for an ever-widening openness to public participation. Farrell comments: "When great hermeneutic theorist Hans Georg Gadamer writes of rhetoric's 'universality,' this is what it seems to intend: the inevitability of and incompleteness of partisanship in every culture at every time. He regards this universality as an ethical problem; whereas we could just as well think of it as an aesthetic promise."[3]

Like justice or the Empire of God, which lures us with a promise of fullness never fully achieved, Caputo's weak theology resists the closure of the same, affirming Derrida's notion of a "productive reading" that "puts [a text] at risk, that exposes its vulnerabilities, that opens it to what it did not see coming."[4] Caputo's weak theology, neither assumes nor aims at a fixed, declarative position, but is a figurative space, a poetic opening that strives to keep discourse open—an opening that embraces the variety of calls from feminist, womanist, liberationist, ecological, and other theologies. His very productive call for shifting from a rationalistic to a *theopoetic* stance has a polemical strategy—that of calling for both personal and cultural transformation which does not long for everlasting, eternal rest but for cultural and political work that practices listening deeply to the suffering of the peoples of the world and the suffering of the earth itself.

Caputo's 2006, *The Weakness of God*, does not follow Derrida's affirmation of debate, above. As we saw in his treatment of the story of the "Man

---

2. Caputo, *Radical Hermeneutics*, 196.
3. Farrell, *Norms of Rhetorical Culture*, 100.
4. Caputo, *Hermeneutics*, 123.

with a Withered Hand," in Mark's gospel, Caputo sees a gap between reason/ mind (*nous*) and the heart (*kardia*)—domains which we have seen him link to strong and weak theology, respectively. In this chapter, I want to explore further what is going on in Caputo's use of these terms, especially for the clusters of strong and weak theology, respectively.

Caputo's fascination with the separation, the gulf, between *nous*, with its needs for order, control, evidence, and argument, and *kardia*, with its more Jewish emphasis on the heart, underscoring receptivity, exposure, and feeling—on being called and claimed by suffering—is explored in multiple places among his texts. Here, in *Against Ethics*, he discusses *phronesis* (practical reason) and situates it somewhat between *nous* and *kardia*.

> *Phronesis* is a mode of *nous*, a matter of practical intelligence, not exactly of having a heart (*kardia*, *misericordia*). *Phronesis* is primarily cognitive; to be sure it is "practical" cognition, but it is still primarily *logos*, *ratio*, and unconcealing. *Phronesis* means being sharp enough to see into the idiosyncrasies of the situation, the subtleties of a complicated and slightly unprecedented situation. The *argumentum ad misericordiam* [or, the argument from compassion] is not a matter of practical intelligence but of a certain succumbing to the claims of the Other, a giving in, a melting, a surrender, a loss of self; not *nous* but *kardia*.[5]

In the same work, Caputo uses the language of "obligation" to get at what he means by *kardia* as "succumbing to the claims of the Other."

> Obligation is . . . a matter of being claimed, in which something has a hold on us, something that is older than us, that has us before we have it. There is nothing subjectivistic about obligation. It is not an effect produced by a subject, not the work of a subject, but rather something produced in me, as in a patient, something that happens to me . . . It is my unflagging supposition that there is something about suffering that stops us in our tracks. The whole idea of a poetics of obligation is to find an idiom for the fact (as it were) that we are laid hold of by others, seized and laid claim to, that the fullness of freedom is hollowed out by the hollow eyes of those who suffer.[6]

It is this sense of being seized, grasped, and moved, especially by suffering, that causes Caputo to claim that the Greek vocabulary of *nous*, *logos*, and *phronesis* does not do justice to the felt experience of being "seized and laid

---

5. Caputo, *Against Ethics*, 117.
6. Caputo, *Against Ethics*, 31–32.

claim to." Hence the need to invoke the capacity not simply to feel for the other, but the capacity to "be grasped by" the other, the capacity to "have a heart."[7] Yet, again, only now in *Weakness*, and alluding back to his treatment of Mark's "Man with a Withered Hand," he writes: "*Kardia* represents a certain 'succumbing,' a surrendering, a '*se rendre*,' giving into, giving oneself over to, the claims of singularity . . . a surrender to the needs of this other one—this poor one, this lame or leper, this withered hand, this justice over and against . . . what is required by the law, which is universal."[8] In contrast to *kardia*, Caputo writes, "Phronesis" is too given to a language of "hard arguments" and "scientific debates," empirical reasoning, and, probability. "*Phronesis*," he writes in *Weakness*, "is the sight that comes from the acquisition of training, of experience, of time and a certain expertise."[9] It is a discourse of planning, strategy, stability, and sovereignty, while weak theology does not seek its own advantage but is responsive to the call of the other.

By using *phronesis* to clarify and further sharpen the difference, the gulf between *nous* and *kardia*, Caputo creates a chasm that needs to be bridged, healed, papered over, as it were, by a new proposal that invents, or calls attention to, an "impractical" dynamic at work over-against strong theology's *phronesis*. Playing parasitically off both Greek and Jewish traditions to re-connect them in a "new *nous*," he invents the term *metanoetics*, which leans away from the tactical knowledge of *nous* and *phronesis* and towards a longing for transformation. "In *metanoetics*, the rule of a strictly cognitive *nous* is broken and replaced by a heart-based nous, a *nous* that in terms of the old physiology would have its seat, not in the head, but in the breast, for indeed the word *phronesis* itself refers to the *phren*, the chest and the heart."[10] By *metanoetics*, Caputo invokes not another rational claim but, instead, a model of truth from the *kardia* side of the house, as it were. A truth not to be *thought* about, but a truth *to be lived-into*. Here, he is decidedly partisan. He is not, in some objective fashion, describing the attributes of one approach to theology with another. He is engaged in an argument, in an appeal, to any readers he might have and to any denominational authorities that might be listening, to imagine transforming the work of theology from defensive arguments over authority to an enlivening invitation to pursue with our lives what Jesus spoke of in the imagery and tropes of the Empire of God. As he writes in his 2007 book *What Would Jesus Deconstruct?*: "Forgiveness

---

7. I can't help but think of Schleiermacher and his notion of "*Gefühl*," his "feeling of absolute dependence", and Langdon Gilkey's discussions of a "felt dimension" to human experience.

8. Caputo, *Weakness of God*, 143.

9. Caputo, *Weakness of God*, 142.

10. Caputo, *Weakness of God*, 142.

and bread, healing hearts and healing bodies, turning all things around in a profound and sweeping *metanoia*, a generalized metanoetics, which means to be of a new mind, a new heart, a new creation, a new order of both spirit and flesh."[11]

FROM PRIORITY OF SELF TO PRIORITY OF THE OTHER

Throughout his many discussions of the relation and differences between *nous* and *kardia*, *phronesis* and *kardia*, Caputo, as we saw in the comparative list of terms in chapter one, aligns *kardia* with a priority on otherness, while aligning *nous* with a more calculating priority on the self/same. Emerging from Caputo's sense of invitation, of "being called," is a radical questioning of the traditional assumptions of ethical priority, namely, that of "self" over "other." The event of a call, for Caputo, always calls us out of ourselves.

> Unlike the garden-variety philosophical views of ethics, which are organized around the autonomous subject . . . the kingdom is organized around what philosophers call "heteronomy," where responsibility means responding to the other; so the self is not an agent but a patient, *an-archic*, not *autarchic* (whence an-ethics). One takes oneself to be always already on the receiving end of the call of the other, always already solicited by the one who comes to me from on high just because he or she is laid low, like the man lying in the road whom the Samaritan encounters.[12]

Letting go of the priority of the self, one is called to respond to the other's need. Caputo's sense of the invitation, indeed of the urgent call—that comes to us, to him and his readers, not from on high but from the ditch—that challenges our assumptions, "producing an event," a *krisis* that awakens and calls us to move beyond our habits of easy, passive reading—comfortable with strong theology's divine protection and closed boundaries—to a destabilized and destabilizing foolishness that acts in response to this unconditional call.[13]

In images, linking a "kingdom of outcasts" to Jesus' preaching of the "Empire of God," Caputo calls readers who have privilege and place in the world to turn their lives towards a more radical justice, a justice forgotten

---

11. Caputo, *What Would Jesus Deconstruct?*, 85.
12. Caputo, *Weakness of God*, 137.
13. Caputo, *What Would Jesus Deconstruct?*, 50.

over centuries of Christian cultural power. In doing so, Caputo signals that he hears the call and the teaching of Jesus as affirming those who have been left out and left at the margins while rejecting those who are currently inside the structures of religious and cultural power.

The "Empire of God" in Caputo's vocabulary is not an ontological/metaphysical reality. As he insists in *Specters*: "Radical theology is political theology; *theopoetics* demands *theopraxis*."[14] Similarly, in *Weakness*, Caputo calls the "kingdom of God" a "hyper-reality," which involves living into and being on the path of a not-yet realized promise that calls to us. It is only by us, readers, responding to the call and enacting/engaging/doing the dynamics of the kingdom that it "becomes true," but never fully so.[15] In Caputo's vocabulary, the *theopoet* remains dependent on the reader for completing the seamless, ongoing action of call and response. And Farrell would remind us of the same on the rhetorical side.

BUT WHAT IF?

In his treatment of the Greek term *phronesis*, Caputo writes, in *Radical Hermeneutics*, that the "hermeneutic conception of *phronesis* presupposes an existing schema, a world already in place." He continues: "It (*phronesis*) is the virtue of applying or appropriating a preexisting paradigm."[16] While there is certainly a skill in such application, *phronesis* operates, for Caputo, in hierarchical fashion, essentially fitting the governing rules to particular situations. It does not work from the bottom up but from the top down. And, in his language of "preexisting paradigm" Caputo means an already-closed system, like the systems of Strong Theology. So, he is saying, in the event of a *krisis* that causes a collapse in that preexisting schema, *phronesis*, itself, is put in crisis. "For then it is not a question of having the skill to apply, but of knowing what to apply. Then we find ourselves brought up short... [and] we need a notion of rationality beyond *phronesis*."[17]

Caputo's analysis of *phronesis* as applying a "pre-existing paradigm," begs the question: but what if that paradigm of a strong theology, as he has shown us, begins to weaken? Indeed, Caputo's entire analysis of strong theology has argued—in keeping with Farrell's "refutative enthymeme"—that

---

14. Caputo, *Specters*, 12.

15. In *The Weakness of God*, Caputo writes: "God is God only if I am welcoming the stranger, only when I *do* the name of God, *facere veritatem*, as when I say 'adieu' to the other, where the *dieu* disappears into the valediction given the other." 272

16. Caputo, *Radical Hermeneutics*, 210–11.

17. Caputo, *Radical Hermeneutics*, 211.

strong theology is, indeed, a paradigm in *krisis*. And, thus, Caputo doesn't think *phronesis* can be of help in responding to that trauma.

But what if *phronesis* is not simply an act of application? What if, as Farrell suggests, *phronesis* is not only a "rhetorical virtue," but an *inventional* one? Farrell asks: "If the point of a practical art is actually to do, rather than to know what is sought as an outcome, then what does rhetoric actually do?"[18] Farrell's emphasis on "doing," what Caputo calls "doing the truth," involves a chiasmic, back-and-forth process of listening and responding that echoes Caputo's language of "call and response," a dynamic nicely captured by the title of Daniel Gross' work, *Being Moved: Rhetoric as the Art of Listening*.[19]

As Farrell reminds us, it is the task of the audience to complete the action initiated by the call of the speaker, just as Caputo reminds readers that a call has not gone out if it has not been heard, nor completed if not acted upon. This is why Farrell treats *phronesis* as a rhetorical virtue. In response to the possible question "Why do we need a separate art (i.e., rhetoric) which treats deliberation as an identifiable discursive form and the audience as 'one who decides,'" Farrell writes: "The answer must be that there is need, at times, to firm up and complete our own reasoning practice through the intervention of competent, interested others. Thus, it is that rhetoric, as distinct from all other arts and modes of inquiry, implements *practical reason* through the complementary participation of someone else: namely, the rhetorical audience"[20]

Farrell's audience runs parallel to Caputo's emphasis on the importance of the reader. To get a sense of how much weight Caputo places on the existential work of the reader, consider this comment from Derrida in response to a question by Richard Kearney during the 2001 conference on *Augustine and Postmodernism*: "That is the question of seriousness again. Literature. Is literature serious? Am I serious? Was I serious when I wrote *Circumfession*? I couldn't tell. It depends on you . . . what I write, is to be signed by the other. It's the other's decision to decide. It's up to the other to decide whether I'm serious or not. If you take me seriously, or if you don't."[21]

A large part of Caputo's suspicion of strong theology and its "hard arguments," "debates," "propositions," and "proposals" is his linkage of these terms to claims of *author-ity* and certainty. By emphasizing hermeneutics he plays to the importance of the reader, and the reader's receptivity. But

18. Farrell, *Norms of Rhetorical Culture*, 72.

19. Gross, *Being Moved*, 20. "While rhetoric as the art of public speaking has been a basic course in higher education for millennia, rarely does a course in the humanities focus on the art of listening."

20. Farrell, *Norms of Rhetorical Culture*, 73 (emphasis added).

21. Derrida in "Roundtable Discussion," *Augustine and Postmodernism*, 38,

if Caputo could listen to Farrell's argument that *phronesis* is an *inventional* art, dependent—like Caputo's own works—on an audience for completion, then he might also see *phronesis* in a new light. *Phronesis* might not be in crisis when an "existing schema" is called into question. It may be that Caputo's discussion of the "parasitic character" of weak theology on strong theology, demonstrates that *phronesis* is not simply captive to "application;" *phronesis*, in Caputo's artful hands, is an inventive and relational art, that moves figuratively, poetically, and rhetorically from theological claims that are essentially closed to a critical and creative re-opening of what has been called theological discourse.

While Caputo shows that strong theology is itself bound to application—deploying the sure-and-certain truths of dogma to limit and shut down discourse deemed in advance to be heretical—he also shows how weak theology, by shifting the discourse of theology from head (*logos*) to heart (*kardia*), can rescue and, perhaps, heal traditions so deeply embedded in defensive postures of power that they no longer speak to a real world.

PHRONESIS AND *PATHOS*

In his 2007 text, *What Would Jesus Deconstruct?*, Caputo, in something of a surprise move to this reader, appears to embrace *phronesis* as a model for "all hermeneutics," a model that places *phronesis* alongside the language of *metanoetics*. In line with that apparent realignment of *phronesis* with *kardia*, he here writes of *phronesis* in terms of "undecidability," judgment, and decision.

> Undecidability ensures that a decision will be the issue of a human 'judgment,' not the application of a rule, which could be done by a computer. The predecessor of undecidability in the history of ethics is not Nietzsche's theory of fictions, but Aristotle's notion of practical reason (*phronesis*), which is the capacity to judge amid shifting and variable circumstances and to bring a schema to bear in an unprecedented situation; *phronesis* is the model for all hermeneutics, for which understanding is always interpretation. While in Aristotle this represents a form of practical "reason," there is also something wonderfully "mad" here—"deconstruction is mad about this kind of justice"... with a kind of divinely deconstructive madness, the way one is a mad fool for the kingdom of God."[22]

---

22. Caputo, *What Would Jesus Deconstruct?*, 67.

Yet, even in this "mad," full embrace of *phronesis*, Caputo ignores the dimension that rhetoric plays in moving persons and communities to decision and action, especially in all those areas of public life and discourse that cannot simply be "answered by a computer."[23]

Insofar as Aristotle himself aligned the art and practice of rhetoric with uncertainty, one would think that Caputo, who spends significant time on Heidegger's understanding of Aristotle's focus on *kinesis* (or, motion) would attend more to Aristotle's *Rhetoric*. For there, Aristotle explores how language moves us, not only through *logos*, as I already noted, but also through *ethos*, and *pathos*.[24] Daniel Gross, in his introductory essay to the collection *Heidegger and Rhetoric*, points to the significance of *pathos* in Heidegger's thought. "For Heidegger the fact that we are subject-to-movement in our belief is precisely what defines us as human . . . Without *pathos* we would lack not only sympathies and antipathies that define community, but also the capacity to absorb the past experiences and future possibilities."[25]

Caputo, to his credit, aligns *kardia* with *pathos* in *Weakness*, saying "*kardia* is precisely *pathos* and sensibility, a communication of flesh with flesh . . . a deep and sensitive *pathos* that suffers with the suffering of the other."[26] Yet, if *pathos* rhymes with *kardia*-like compassion, might not rhetoric, in its inventive, kinetic capacity, be compatible with Caputo's understanding of *metanoetics* as a "new *nous*," capable of bleeding over and into the life of *kardia*? In his "Short Precise of *The Weakness of God* and *The Insistence of God*," Caputo may leave such a path open. "The audacity of weak theology is to be, without further pretense, a poetics—a constellation of metaphors and metonymies, of rhetorical tropes and unexpected linguistic turns, of narratives, allegories, and parables, whose cumulative effect is to give words to an underlying form of life."[27] If he can allow for "rhetorical tropes" to contribute to his theopoetic project, then perhaps *phronesis*, reclaimed as an *inventional* art, can partner, as it were, with his *metanoetics*, to aid in the process of liberating his readers from the illusory confines of strong theology.

---

23. Caputo, *What Would Jesus Deconstruct?* 67.
24. See Caputo, *Weakness of God*, 144.
25. Gross, *Heidegger and Rhetoric*, 36.
26. Caputo, *Weakness of God*, 144.
27. Caputo, "Short Precis," 3.

5

Drawing Us In and Calling Us Out

AN INVITATIONAL RHETORIC

Caputo writes in *Weakness* that in contrast to strong, official, authorized power, the Empire of God "belongs to the sphere of invitation," and "invitation is a weak force," offering "another way to be."[1] In both *Weakness* and *Insistence*, in contrast to strong theology's focus on "presence" and official "power," Caputo invites his readers to "suppose" a wholly different set of theological, or better, *theopoetic* possibilities that might free them "from being's chains."[2] Here are just a few of many possible examples:

> Suppose we abandon the top-down schema of one Father Almighty, one king to rule the land (another father), in favor of a paradigm where such power slips out of favor?
>
> Suppose we say that the event that is sheltered in the name of God does not belong to the order of power and presence, but rather withdraws from the world in order to station him or herself ... with everything that the world despises ...
>
> Suppose God most especially pitches his (sic) tent among the homeless, so that God has no place on which to lay his (sic) head.
>
> Suppose further, that "religion" and "theology," which are human, all too human and not to be confused with God, tend systematically, structurally, regularly, to forget this, and to associate themselves with a discourse of power?

---

1. Caputo, *Weakness of God*, 15–16.
2. Talk about polemical!

> Suppose that we reverse these gears and thrust theology in
> the direction of weakness and the disavowal of power?[3]

In these and many more rhetorical "supposes," Caputo calls forth a response from his readers, an active willingness to stay with him. He seeks to find, as well as to build a following, an audience that will not simply run off when strong theology flexes its omnipotent muscles.

Caputo's use of "suppose" and "perhaps" are good examples of what Sonja K. Foss and Cindy L. Griffin call "invitational rhetoric." "Unlike persuasive discourse," they write, "which aggressively seeks to change people's minds," invitational rhetoric "enables rhetors to disengage from the dominance of mastery so common to a system of oppression and to create a reality of equality and mutuality in its place."[4] Caputo writes of his own style: "Instead of producing a strong theology that describes a great ontotheological generator supplying endless energy to the world, I produce a charged field where sparks are thrown off in every direction, constituting the divine disturbance I will shortly describe as a 'sacred anarchy.'"[5]

Caputo invites readers to disengage from the mastery of strong theologies and to consider, with an open mind, a weak theology of possibilities, of sparks, and of allegedly "modest proposals," which, in the spirit of Jonathan Swift, suddenly do not seem so modest. Caputo's weak polemic invites readers away from the assertive, traditional dogmatic claims of classical and modern theology, and towards the creative energy of the poetic (coming from the Latin, *poein*, "to make"), with its sense of being addressed, of being called, of being called to respond and to act.

In his invitational language of "suppose" and "perhaps," Caputo lures his readers into a parabolic enactment of his call-and-response liturgy. As he calls his readers to imagine the shift from a strong theology to a weak theology, he invites us to experience the event of receiving a call—even as we read—that invites, calls for our response to not only re-imagine but to change our lives. What Michael Ure, in his article, "Michel Foucault's Rhetorical Practice: the 1961 Preface to History and Madness," says about the style of Foucault's Preface, namely that it "use[s] rhetoric to cultivate an experience that tempts them" (i.e., readers) "to transform their lives," can be easily said of Caputo as well. As Ure writes: "Foucault's 1961 Preface does

---

3. Caputo, *Weakness of God*, 33.
4. See Rollins, "Persuasion's Ethical Force," 2–8.
5. Caputo, *Weakness of God*, 13. It was Dieter Georgi, at Harvard Divinity School in the 1908s who, in his emphasis on democracy, noted that "anarchy," in Greek, simply means "without a head." And thus, he would say he was very comfortable being an anarchist.

not conform to the model of the sovereign author who commands readers to correctly interpret the text according to his intentions, but, . . . constitutes a lyrical invitation to 'cultivate [their] legitimate strangeness.'"[6]

By positioning us readers as receivers, as the audience of a call, always already addressed to us, and thus, also as readers responding to a text, Caputo seeks to move us, his readers, to embrace his—or is it "God's"?—invitation to transformation.

In *Weakness*, Caputo encourages readers to hear Jesus' preaching of the Empire of God in light of his (Caputo's) language of a "call without a caller": "The kingdom of God is an event that commands us on its own merits, whoever is its ontic author, like a beautiful poem from centuries ago whose author is now completely unknown. In that sense the death of the author, which would mean here the death of God, is the narrow gate through which we reach the kingdom of God."[7] That "text" might be the New Testament or Hebrew Bible, or perhaps another text, a novel or poem, or even, perhaps one of Caputo's frail works. In this appeal from "ontic-author" Caputo, one can hear a call to shift one's lens of interpretation from a focus on metaphysical reason and the authority of authors—including the traditional authority ascribed to "God" as the author of creation, and/or the New Testament—to a poetics of the event that reimagines reading the New Testament as an invitation.

> A poetics is not true the way a scientific theory is true, as a covering law that is weakened, altered, or refuted by the accumulated weight of evidence and replaced by a competing scientific theory. A poetics is true with the truth of the event; it wants to *become true, to make itself true, to make itself come true*, to be transformed into truth, so that its truth is a species of truth as *facere veritatem*.[8]

Caputo's language on interpreting the New Testament as a poetics, as an *event* that wants to become true, that longs to be lived out, rather than posing as claims that call for our true belief, is to hold out, in one's reading of the Scriptures, for the possibility of receiving a call upon one's life.[9]

6. Ure, "Michel Foucault's Rhetorical Practice," 163.

7. Caputo, *Weakness*, 116. On the topic of the "death of the author," see the work of Roland Barthes, among others.

8. Caputo, *Weakness of God*, 118. *Facere veritatem* means "to do truth."

9. See Caputo, *Weakness of God*, 119. "In virtue of the transformation into the event, we stop thinking of the Scriptures as handing over a string of supernatural assertions whose truth lies in their correspondence to supernatural facts too far off or too high up for us to see with our unaided eyes . . . and we start thinking of them as invitations to transform our lives" (emphasis added).

In and through Caputo's invitational rhetoric he constructs on the page a proposal, a "perhaps" that wants to "become true," not only on the page but off the page and in our lives. He longs and prays that his work—weak and invisible as it is—might be a vehicle in which what is going on under the name of "God" becomes active and real, moving readers to live in an impossibly different, more open, Joycean "chaosmos."

What begins as a rhetoric of invitation, as an aesthetic supposition—of "perhaps," or "imagine,"—moves the reader, once moved, hooked, or even seduced, as Kierkegaard might prefer—to a more serious discourse of obligation, and thence to a yet more profound leap of decision, transformation, and faith.[10]

Caputo's call without a caller is not simply a poetic but rhetorical construct, shaping the urgency as well as the "partialist"—neither complete nor objective—character of the call. Noting that "rhetoric is avowedly partialist in the way it views issues, the world, and the other," Farrell writes: "But if rhetoric is biased toward the partialist stance, a larger possibility can be claimed for it where ethics are concerned. We are drawn to our larger obligation to the innocent victim, the needy stranger, by our ability, as Schopenhauer sensed, to see the other in ourselves." Farrell's emphasis on the priority of "obligation," acting on what he calls our "complicity in the interests of others," is similar to Caputo's emphasis on obligation in the quotation from *Against Ethics*, I used above. Yet, Caputo's emphasis on the priority of the other is more emphatic than Farrell's. It is the suffering of the other, that "seizes us."

> Obligation is . . . a matter of being claimed, in which something has a hold on us, something that is older than us, that has us before we have it . . . It is my unflagging supposition that there is something about suffering that stops us in our tracks. The whole idea of a poetics of obligation is to find an idiom for the fact (as it were) that we are laid hold of by others, seized and laid claim to, that the fullness of freedom is hollowed out by the hollow eyes of those who suffer.[11]

Caputo's partialist stance invites us, calls us, in this passage to be grasped and moved by a suffering "that stops us in our tracks." While Caputo longs for suffering to stop us so that we might be moved, and in turn, move differently, I have to ask: Does it? What happens when, by our "hardness of heart," we become inured to the suffering of homeless people, for example,

---

10. I think here of Kierkegaard's ladder, as it were, from the aesthetic, to the ethical, to the religious. For a discussion of these see his book *Stages on Life's Way*.

11. Caputo, *Against Ethics*, 32.

or to the suffering of those seeking to escape from the political violence of their countries by entering—out of desperation—the United States? It is, I suggest, the forcefulness of Caputo's rhetoric that "stops us in our tracks" and haunts us, that calls us back to that primal openness to the Other, which we have all too easily forgotten.[12]

If readers follow Caputo's call to imagine risking their lives for others in response to his theopoetic proposal, they are, in effect, choosing to enter a process of possible persuasion and transformation. There is the possibility that in response to a call—a call one might hear in the New Testament or in the pages of Augustine, or Kierkegaard, Keller, or, perhaps even, Caputo—one will be moved, called, to change one's life, entering upon the "way of the cross." Don Compier, in *What is Rhetorical Theology?* quotes Frank Lentriccia, who argued that "the point is not only to interpret texts but in interpreting them, to change our society."[13]

IN A WEAK CALL, A WEAKER REVELATION

Caputo's invitational language of "call and response" is not simply a phrase drawing on the energy of jazz and the moving liturgy of the black church, as rich as those traditions are, but is itself a bold re-imagination of the classic Christian topics of revelation and faith. Revelation, here, for Caputo, is no longer envisioned as a transcendent Truth that sets up, in turn, the faithful's response of right belief. Instead, this contextual call, or small "r" revelation, calls and invites the reader to a public response which enacts and makes the call true by carrying it out "in the world." In keeping with the emerging image cluster that gathers around weakness, Caputo's reimagination of revelation as the event of a call, underscores its "receptive," "vulnerable," and "responsive" character in contrast to strong theology's claims to dogmatic truth.

This "revelation," if you will, calls the reader at once out of a profoundly hard-hearted world, but also "back into the world" with courageous and hopeful work to do.[14] Caputo writes in *Weakness* about reimagining the revelatory character of the Scriptures through this revised lens of a lowercase revelation.

---

12. The difference between these two perspectives may be captured in "The Last Judgement" parable in Matthew 25, when those who are condemned respond, "But when did *we* see *you*, Jesus, and not respond to *you*?" They don't think it was a fair test. Such is the way of calculation.

13. Compier, *What is Rhetorical Theology?*, 25.

14. See Plato's Myth of the Cave at the beginning of book 7 of *The Republic* for that double movement of being called/pulled out of the world and then "sent back into the world."

> The sacred texts are treated, not as Divine Revelation that definitively props up the authority of some confessional faith or ecclesiastical office, nor as the record of some extraordinary empirical event from long ago that tells us *wie es eigentlich gewesen ist*, (or, how it actually was) as if human history was literally launched six thousand years ago by two painfully naked and parentless people who made the big mistake of being drawn into a conversation with a sneaky snake . . . For these texts are solicitations, appeals coming from I know not where about a way to be, a style of existence, about a poetic possibility that we are invited to transform into existential actuality.[15]

The language of "solicitation," "invitation," and "appeal" that Caputo uses to undertake a "transformation" to a new way of being is not simply poetic or figurative language; it is rhetorical language that artfully draws, urges, and coaxes readers, to respond. Caputo continues: "The sacred text thus undergoes a twofold transformation: first, into the event of the call; and then the call, in turn, is transformed into existential reality."[16]

But again, that "call" is not "transformed into existential reality" unless and until "we" readers/hearers are moved by it and enact it in the world. This is why Caputo says that there is no revelation unless it is heard and acted upon; just as there is no call if there is no response. "The truth of the event is a deed, something to do, to translate into the flesh of existence. To be in the truth means to be transformed by a call, to have been turned around, to have been given a new heart."[17]

If we choose to follow such a call, such an ungrounded invitation, the goal of such a path will not be found in the tradition of right belief. Rather, says Caputo, it will be found in taking up the difficulty of living from one's "heart" and turning towards the suffering of public life, responding to the revelatory event of the call with a testimony of commitment, of living, and giving active witness. For it is only by loving and welcoming the unexpected, the stranger, responding in the name of the "God" who loves the stranger, that "God," Caputo says, can "become "God" . . . "the name of 'God' must be translated into an event, and the event must be translated into a deed."[18] He continues:

---

15. Caputo, *Weakness of God*, 117.
16. Caputo, *Weakness of God*, 117.
17. Caputo, *Weakness of God*, 16.
18. Caputo, *Weakness of God*, 272. See also p. 114: "In the hermeneutic situation from which I set out, we are all constituted as the recipients of a call about whose origin we cannot comment with assurance, a call floating out over the abyss of the radical hermeneutical fix we are in. The call is itself constituted by being heard, and being heard

> The translation is radical, beyond any semantic transfer, beyond any aligning of meanings in different semantic fields, beyond being and knowledge, because it is translated into witnessing, into action . . . It is necessary to rid ourselves of God in order to witness to God.[19]

To engage in the practice and work of weak theology, according to Caputo, is to enter into a vulnerability that exposes oneself to radical uncertainty. It requires an embrace of uncertainty and vulnerability all the way down. In this way, Caputo's invitational rhetoric not only mirrors but enacts on the page, the luring character of the existential call that insists on a response.[20] It is a type of literary onomatopoeia, of the text enacting or doing—luring the reader—just as "Justice" or "God" existentially lures law and religion into the future, weaving the two levels of call and response tightly together. "Theology," he writes, "is not about making propositional claims but about being claimed, not about proposing but about being exposed to something that is beyond the reach of propositions."[21] Once again, Caputo aligns rhetoric and debate in sharp contrast to weak theology's emphasis on "being claimed" and "being exposed." Yet, he also turns to the language of "persuasion" to hold out hope for the difference that the weak force of radical theology can make. Persuasion can move us—not to certainty—but more importantly to decision and to action, crying out, "Yes, Yes." In response to being called to make the leap, not of knowledge but, of courageous transformation, we open our hearts and turn to heal the suffering of others.

One of the many things I have in mind by using Farrell's phrase that rhetoric is how things "come to matter," involves bringing possibilities to matter, that is to say, to existence and embodiment, to deeds in the diverse spaces of public life. Two passages, one from Bob Funk and the other from John Dominic Crossan will clarify the difficulty of this leap, of this decision. First, Funk, from his introduction to *The Five Gospels*.

> Academic folk are a retiring lot. We prefer books to lectures, and solitude to public display. Nevertheless, we have too long buried

---

is in turn constituted by our responding, by our heeding, and not simply hearing, or by our hearing as heeding." See also page 273: "Witnessing is not a thought but a 'deed.'"

19. Caputo, *Weakness of God*, 272.

20. See Caputo, *Weakness of God*, 113–15, in which he articulates the "hermeneutic preunderstanding" of the experiment that is *Weakness*. "Theology, any theology, weak or strong, is the explication of the event that is implicit in the name of God, from God knows where, from something I know not what—from God, from some World-Soul, or from a dark corner of the unconscious—soliciting us from afar and calling us beyond ourselves."

21. See Caputo, *Specters of God*, 22.

> our considered views of Jesus and the gospels in technical jargon and in obscure journals. We have hesitated to contradict TV evangelists and pulp religious authors for fear of political reprisal and public controversy. And we have been intimidated by promotion and tenure committees to whom the charge of popularizing or sensationalizing biblical issues is anathema. It is time for us to quit the library and speak up.[22]

Funk locates scholars within a Heideggerian sense of conventionality with its reticence to enter the fray of the political.

And then Crossan, writing at the end of his Prologue to *Jesus: A Revolutionary Biography*:

> I conclude by reproducing here an imaginary dialogue . . . The Historical Jesus is speaking to me:
> "I've read your book, Dominic, and it's quite good. So now you're ready to live by my vision and join me in my program?"
> "I don't think I have the courage, Jesus, but I did describe it quite well, didn't I? And the method was especially good, wasn't it?"
> "Thank you, Dominic, for not falsifying the message to suit your own incapacity. That is at least something."
> "Is it enough, Jesus?"
> "No, Dominic, it is not."[23]

The leap from brilliant hermeneutics, from interpretation and understanding to engaged action is a vast one, as vast as the leap from Kierkegaard's "ethical" stage to that of the "religious." And for Funk, as for Crossan, there is in these reported failures a sense of both the profound difficulty in risking that leap, but also of the felt obligation to make it. In Funk's final lines, as well as in the "historical Jesus'" words to Crossan, one hears the acknowledgment of the habits and the fears, the "hardness of heart," that systemically keep us from doing all that the way of Jesus calls forth from us.

---

22. Funk, *The Five Gospels*, 34.
23. Crossan, *Jesus: A Revolutionary Biography*, xiv.

6

The Shape of a Call That Moves Us

IN THE PREVIOUS TWO chapters, I have begun discussing several theological moves by which Caputo develops his theopoetic proposal. As I have touched upon Caputo's shift to understanding Scripture as solicitation and his re-imagination of revelation and faith, I have begun to approach an interconnected set of topics—or "moves" as I prefer to say—that constitute the rhetorical, and often quite invisible, dynamics of a theological proposal.

By focusing on the persuasive, rhetorical character of Caputo's work I do not mean to undermine his attention to either radical hermeneutics or *theopoetics*, but only to demonstrate the profoundly rhetorical dimension of his hermeneutics and poetics. As he takes his radical interpretations of Christian theology into public discourse in hopes of persuading ecclesial and public audiences to reimagine faith (*foi*) and to live into that new understanding, he moves beyond hermeneutics and into the work of rhetoric. His hermeneutics, I am suggesting, is always already "wired-up" to a rhetorical effort that confronts the abuses of strong theology and its inclinations to arrogance and violence.

In their book, *Everything's an Argument*, Andrea A. Lunsford and John J. Ruszkiewicz include a chapter on proposals in which they note three main characteristics of proposal-type discourse: First, "[t]hey call for change, often in response to a problem." Second, "they focus on the future." Third, "[t]hey center on the audience."[1] In previous chapters, we have seen Caputo engage each of these three elements. While I appreciate Lunsford's and Ruszkiewicz's

---

1. Lunsford and Ruszkiewicz, *Everything's an Argument*, 274ff.

discussion, I suggest that political and theological proposals have something of a yet richer rhetorical structure, closer to five topics than to three.

Using the acceptance speeches by the nominees at major political party conventions in the U.S., I have shown in a variety of pieces, how those speeches tend to move/work through five major theo-political topics, that together, interactively, construct a proposal, or solicitation, for their readers/listeners to consider. Those moves include 1) affirmation of the audience's capacity for goodness, 2) the turning away from that capacity with tragic consequences, 3) the healing of that brokenness and renewal of that initial capacity, 4) the renewal of communal belonging and the significance of participation that seeks to restore the initial affirmation, to 5) pursuit of a vision that draws us toward transformation and the future, calling forth again the audience's capacity for goodness.[2]

Elsewhere I have proposed that the topics of a constructive theology are not *sui generis* Christian but share with political discourse a common, rhetorical/proposal structure, call it a complex trope of leadership. For if we think of tropes as a "kind of plot device," then the interconnectedness of these five topics across methods and models of theological construction, enacts the persuasive movement of the text.[3] Thus, these five moves are best understood not as stand-alone "topics" but, in their interaction together, as aspects of an *inventional* process that seeks to move a political or theological audience to risk commitment and action on behalf of the person and work of the "chosen" candidate, or, in the case of Christian theology, to live out of the vision and practice of Jesus, as proposed by the theologian.[4]

Caputo has emphasized throughout his work that it is not the *name*, "God" that matters but what is "astir in the name of 'God.'" Similarly, we can ask: "What is astir in the topic/name of humanity "created in the image of 'God?'" "What is astir in the topic/name of sin?" "What is astir, or going on in the topic/name and work of Christ?" "What is astir in the name "church"

---

2. See Appendix II analyzing the five moves in Bill Clinton's 1992 Democratic Convention address, taken from a longer essay published in *The Fourth R.*, September (33.5) 2022, 3–7; 22. As I discuss there, it sometimes occurs—in both theological and political proposals—that the text will skip over the first topic of affirmation because the author feels the need to emphasize the crisis or problem that the community must urgently address.

3. See the opening page of the following: Book Tropes: The Ultimate List of 70+ Tropes in Literature (scribophile.com), accessed June 27, 2024.

4. By using the terms "person" and "work" I play off the two Christological emphases on the "person" and "work" of the Christ. I do so because in the overlapping structure of these speeches, the newly anointed candidate presents their proposal to lead the party to victory, over against the "fallen" forces of the opposition, in Christ-like fashion.

that seeks to live out Jesus' vision of the Empire of God?" and, "What is astir in that name of the *eschaton*, of the promise for which we long, but which may not come, or come in ways we did not expect? In dealing with each of these topics, Caputo plays parasitically off Christian traditions in shaping a new theopoetic proposal.

Yet, in addition, one needs to ask: "What is going on in the interaction of these moves/topics? The topics are not hermeneutically or rhetorically static, but they interpret one another such that how one interprets one topic shapes the way one interprets the other topics. Think of the list of terms we drew up to capture Caputo's discussion of strong and weak theologies, back in chapter one. These terms contribute to Caputo's proposal as it takes shape in and through his drawing upon those terms to shape his interpretation of the five topics. At issue here is not formal coherence, but more importantly, the felt, moving character of the proposal—the way it builds not only cognitive but emotive force in the work of invitation and persuasion.

What is astir in the dynamic movement among the topics, is not finally a propositional, or doctrinal claim, but a play of words seeking to move readers and listeners who are open to being moved—open perhaps to making a decision and commitment to live into a proposed vision of the Empire of God. In the remainder of this chapter, I turn primarily to Caputo's 2013 work, *The Insistence of God*, to explore further what I am calling, the rhetorical dimension of his *theopoetic* project, which he here names as a "radical theology." While I have been talking about the rhetorical interconnectedness of those five topics, it is important to note that these topics, or names of topics, are not anything like a fixed structure. By speaking of a rhetorical structure, I mean to point to a dynamic that is itself in flux. To that point, Caputo does not explicitly name the five topics I just mentioned. That he does not use those names suggests to me that he wants out of the classical game of theology and the way those topics can bind and close down the "truth," closing out the suffering of the world. Indeed, he seems bored by their plodding predictability as found in many confessional and constructive theologies. And yet, just because he does not name them, doesn't mean they are not there.

Here, I will use Caputo's language of "what's going on in the name of those topics," to feel my way into his proposal, to grasp the textures and moves of his poetics that haunt and trade off the classical content of those very topics. I believe Caputo's proposal—the gift of his complex argument—can revive and revise these staid topics into more dynamic moves that can capture our imaginations anew. Perhaps more importantly, we will see that Caputo's interpretation/construction of what is going on in the name of "God," emerges within the play of these five topics calling us to transformation.

Even as he does not use those explicit topics to mark the shifts within his proposal, the underlying dynamic of those moves keeps calling him out, as it were, and it becomes clear, as one moves with him, that he doesn't want completely out of the theological gambit. He wants out in an in-ish sort of way. He wants in in an out-ish sort of way. He wants to start some trouble, and the gift of his work does just that.

What if? he asks. What if we started with "perhaps?" And that is where I pick up his text, in its opening pages, beginning with the contours of this land of perhaps as the vital context for his interpretation of these topics. Caputo begins his book with three solid pages offering a variety of interpretations of the word "perhaps," suggestively shaping the meaning of the term as he goes.[5] Here are several that give a hopeful shape to the word that is so important to his project.

"'Perhaps' is not the safety of indecision but a radical risk, for nothing guarantees that things will turn out well, that what is coming will not be a disaster. 'Perhaps' is not paralysis but the fluid milieu of undecidability in which every radical decision is made, by which I mean a decision that is not merely programmed or dictated by circumstances." And this one: "The un-certainty of 'perhaps' does not constitute a defect, a failure to attain certainty, but a release from the rule of the certain, an emancipation from the block that certainty throws up against thinking or desiring otherwise. 'Perhaps' galvanizes another kind of thinking."[6]

Unlike the word doubt, which also operates in the region of uncertainty, and which has a longer pedigree in the areas of philosophy and theology, "perhaps," in Caputo's sense, leans into uncertainty precisely to engage it, and not hold back as doubt tends to do. He wants his readers to begin to feel at home with an uncertainty that opens the closed "rule of the certain," and underscores throughout the importance of possibility. Here, "perhaps" has a solicitous, luring character to it. This is why Caputo's proposal is up to some trouble. He has no intention of beginning his work by affirming the truth of the creed and informing us how he will go about explaining what it means for us today. No, drawing on the humility of the word "perhaps" he

---

5. In this chapter I rely primarily on Caputo's *The Insistence of God: A Theology of Perhaps*. While I can and will refer to his book *The Weakness of God* (2006) and other texts including *What Would Jesus Deconstruct* (2007), I think the proposal he makes in *Insistence* is more challenging. His book *The Folly of God: A Theology of the Unconditional* (2016) extends his argument in *Insistence*. See also Caputo's essay: "A Short Précis of *The Weakness of God* and *Insistence of God*."

6. Caputo, *Insistence of God*, 6.

will argue that the creed, and its claims to certainty, is the problem. And that one little word, perhaps, functions to open an alternative proposal, reclaiming those five topics/moves to articulate a faith that engages the realism and intensity of an uncertain world.

For Caputo, "perhaps" is not a term of confusion, indecision, lazy thinking, or simply being "on the fence." Instead, amid uncertainty, "perhaps" is analogous to Paul Tillich's language of being on the boundary, staying open to the genuine uncertainty and undecidability of life.[7] In a world where uncertainty has become the only certain thing, perhaps represents the appropriate stance of both intellectual humility and moral courage.

Having teased us, rhetorically, into an interest in what the language of perhaps might mean for theology, Caputo unpacks the new awareness of uncertainty that haunts all our claims to knowledge and truth. Caputo's perhaps invites us to cross over and to move beyond the land of certainty and right belief to a space and language of "uncertainty," that calls for a new understanding of faith as doing, as practice. If he can persuade us of the importance of making that move, then new ways of enacting community and of moving into the future become open to us, calling for the risk of our response, the risk of our "yes." The call, the proposal within Caputo's solicitation of perhaps, unfolds in the dynamic of the five topics, or moves, we have been discussing. Within the play of what is astir in those five topics we will learn, in a new way, what is astir in the name of God.

DEEP AFFIRMATION—FIRST MOVE

In the face of radical uncertainty, Caputo affirms the capacity for human persons to be open and responsive to their world, to say "perhaps" in a way that leans into the world, and to be hospitable to the event of the unexpected, to welcome the stranger—even in the midst of a fear that may be well-founded.

> A disturbing visitation in the night is an uncertainty in which all the sting of perhaps and a theology of insistence is both modeled and put into play. Hospitality means to say "come" in response to what is calling, and that may well be trouble.

He continues:

> We might say that hospitality is an example of an event, but if so it is an exemplary one, a paradigm, maybe even a surname for any and every event, which can come at any moment, like a

---

7. Tillich, *On the Boundary*, 13.

wayfarer in need of a cup of cold water unless, perhaps, he is a thief in the night.[8]

Hospitality amidst uncertainty is crucial to Caputo's proposal. Precisely because an event is, by definition, what we do *not* see coming, the capacity for hospitality is the capacity to be moved, to be vulnerable to what we cannot see or know. By speaking of the wayfarer's "need of a cup of cold water," Caputo invites us to hear the story of Matthew 25, "I was thirsty, and you gave me something to drink."

Such interruptive calls, like that of the stranger, occur in daily life—a request out of the blue—and those moments might well harbor more than just that literal request. Beyond the request of the moment is the request for a more sustained openness to the stranger and a disposition to risk oneself. Perhaps, what we mean when we speak of "God," is a call to open our lives more widely to the world. Caputo writes: "Hospitality in its paradigmatic sense requires putting ourselves at risk instead of creating a closed circle of "the same," namely of those friends we already know and trust."[9]

By encouraging this capacity for hospitality Caputo says he is "not calling for stupidity but for a judgment that is willing to take a risk."[10] "Things only get interesting," he notes, . . ." [h]ospitality kicks into high gear (becomes "unconditional") when it is impossible . . . when . . . we are asked to welcome the unwelcome; otherwise we are just admitting the same."[11] As long as we know who's coming, (e.g., someone we know and love) then opening our door when they knock does not involve any real risk, does not stretch us towards the neighbor. Drawing on Derrida's play on words, "*hostipitality*," which incorporates the Greek *hostis*, for "stranger," and which further includes the sense of "hostility," Caputo says it is that unknown knocking in the night that can set our hearts racing with anxiety and dread. Yet, it is also in that moment that one can imagine, and enact, the kind of world we dream of and long for, a dream of a wider, more just community.

Action in the face of the undecideable situation matters profoundly. And, thus, again, what is at issue in the event of hospitality is more than the literal request; it is the deeper revelation of whether we are turned primarily inward in fear or outward in courageous engagement. In the event of the call, we receive again and again the opportunity to reach beyond ourselves and care for others and our world. This first topic affirms the goodness of humanity by locating humanity's capacity for difference, for the call of the Other.

8. Caputo, *Insistence of God*, 39.
9. Caputo, *Insistence of God*, 40.
10. Caputo, *Insistence of God*, 41.
11. Caputo, *Insistence of God*, 39.

Precisely because the event is unforeseeable and interruptive, uncertain as to whether it bodes us well or ill, the capacity to say, "Come," to say, "Yes," to that which is uncertain, exposes the human person to ambiguity and danger in a way that cannot be foreclosed. Yet, this is the distinctive characteristic of the human person, namely, to be able to risk a yes to the unknown. "The failure to be certain," writes Caputo, "is not a failure but a "negative capability," a power to sustain the uncertainty that structures the insistence of hospitality."[12] And that negative capability is vital to the practice of hospitality. "Hospitality is not a character trait of the pious, not just a virtue to be cultivated, or one of the several virtues, but the field in which everything we do transpires. Hospitality describes not a particular part but the very structure or movement of life, not our "essence" but the explanation for why every attempt to prescribe our essence is always already outstripped."[13] Why outstripped? Because hospitality is the paradigm of engaging what we cannot see coming. The capacity for responsiveness resists the closure of a defined essence and insists on the capacity of natality, of the new, impossible birth that is to come.

Just as in conventional theology, where to be created in the "image of God" is to possess a capacity for Truth—by virtue of possessing a rational soul—and that transcendent truth is "God"—so, too the capacity to risk ourselves, to welcome the stranger, to say yes to "God, perhaps," might itself be what is going on in that name of the *Imago Dei*. "The name (of) 'God' harbors the omnipresent beckoning of the 'perhaps,' like a spirit that insists and insinuates itself into everything, that breathes where it will, the possibility of an impossibility that inheres in still and small things. God does not exist; God is a spirit that calls, a spirit than can happen anywhere and haunts everything, insistently."[14]

The responsiveness that Caputo interprets as "the very structure, the movement of life," opens onto the call—without a caller!—that calls each of us to reach beyond ourselves and into trouble. "Think of God as a divine stranger who needs food, shelter, and clothing, where the insistence of God is in need of our assistance."[15] In this suggestion, "God" is not a ruling, eternal deity, but "God" is at risk in the midst of the world. The capacity for hospitality that is at the heart of who we are is always already an openness to a call that is going on in the name of "God." To be open to the unexpected call is itself a capacity to be lured, to be "beckoned," to be drawn out of ourselves.

---

12. Caputo, *Insistence of God*, 40.
13. Caputo, *Insistence*, of God, 43.
14. Caputo, *Insistence of God*, 13.
15. Caputo, *Insistence of God*, 42–43.

It is vital at this point to reiterate that when Caputo writes of risk, he is not asking us to risk belief in an eternal, unchanging transcendent God. Instead, he writes of the call—the insistent call—to risk ourselves, our bodies, for another, for the stranger, for the earth, in whom we just may meet "God," or not. "The stranger is both a venerable figure and dangerous, risky business, putting the circle of the same at risk. Without the risk, it is just more of the same. The stranger is maddening, trouble, like God; undecidable, like God. Are strangers and undecidability figures of God? Or is God, perhaps, a figure of the undecidability of the stranger, of openness to the other?"[16] Here the political and the theological overlap. Caputo's impossible event of "God" will not take us out of this world and out of trouble but draw us more deeply into the world and into its troubles. "But in radical theology we make room for another trauma, the bracing trauma of the event, of the other person, and of everything *tout autre*, which assaults our narcissism and draws us out of ourselves. If the name of God is not causing us a great deal of difficulty, it is not God we are talking about."[17] This is why Caputo writes: "I pray the God who exposes me to trouble to rid me of the God who keeps me safe, who functions as a guarantor of tranquility and order."[18] As we will see, "faith," in Caputo's proposal goes looking for trouble in the world; it is not a "belief" that stamps one's ticket, as it were, out of this world. Why does it go looking for trouble? Because "the name of God is the name of trouble."[19]

CRISIS, THE THREATENING PROBLEM— SECOND MOVE

The act of courage, writes Caputo, emerges only in the act of responsiveness. Exposure to the event, to the uncertain, "to trouble," is the condition of the possibility for hospitality. Caputo underscores the real risks—as well as the real courage—involved in practicing hospitality. Given the presence of fear, this capacity often—most often—turns towards affirming "the same" rather than risking hospitality towards "the other." It is this tendency to turn inward in response to the event of the unexpected that Caputo locates the threatening problem, as I call it—the tendency for not only individuals but also institutions and confessional traditions to forget the distinction, the gap between the insistent call of the promise of "God, perhaps," and their own doctrinal beliefs. "In them [confessional churches] the infinitival event

---

16. Caputo, *Insistence of God*, 42.
17. Caputo, *Insistence of God*, 28.
18. Caputo, *Insistence of God*, 43
19. Caputo, *Insistence of God*, 39.

is contracted to a finite and historical content, an identifiable form that has a proper name, that is inextricably embedded in the contingency of its particular cultural form of life."[20]

In his 1978 book, *The Mystical Element in Heidegger's Thought*, Caputo writes that Heidegger "sees in reason something analogous to pride, an obstinate self-sufficiency, a willfulness, a desire to impose its own categories on things . . . The fault of the metaphysician is 'false pride.'"[21] Caputo follows suit, to some extent, in his later works, finding in the metaphysical and evangelical proclamations of Christian dogma and Christian superiority, a willful ignorance and dishonesty, a falseness—what he calls "rouge theology"—still clinging to the modern delusion of rational truth.[22] Indeed, Caputo finds in the tendency of confessional theologies to cling to worldviews now gone, the *hubris* of sin.

To be sure, Caputo affirms the existence of confessional theologies, insofar as they themselves were once historical responses to the infinitival call that cannot be named. The problem is that they conveniently forgot that their claims were contingent and localized. By forgetting that distinction, "the confessional traditions have a built-in tendency to close ranks, to close the circle, to make things easy for themselves, to excommunicate the 'perhaps it could be otherwise.'"[23] By proclaiming that these confessional claims are themselves foundational and absolute, such theologies fail to live up to the "radical honesty" required for Caputo's understanding of radical theology.[24] "I posit that there are midnight moments when confessional theologians toss and turn with the haunting thought that what they call a gift of grace is in fact an accident of birth—that, had they been born in another time and place, they would have entirely different theologies."[25] These confessional theologies, says Caputo, are caught, giving themselves over to nostalgia for a set of assumptions—philosophical, political, cultural—that are no more, but still held onto by congregations assured of their absolute, unchanging truth. Insofar as church leaders see theology as an "answering" tradition, they tend to see their responsibility as one of reassuring and securing the believing community, casting suspicions on scientific findings and secular

20. Caputo, *Insistence of God*, 85.

21. Caputo, *Mystical Element in Heidegger*, 176.

22. This view of rhetoric shows up not only in passages discussing the "rouging" of theology in *Weakness* but also in conversation. Personal conversation with Jack Caputo in Salt Lake City, May 24, 2024. The "rouging" imagery is itself problematic as it tends to victimize those who must make their economic livelihood on the streets as sex workers.

23. Caputo, *Insistence of God*, 85.

24. Caputo, *Insistence of God*, 72.

25. Caputo, *Insistence of God*, 72.

culture, while simultaneously calling people to conversion, to the harbor of safety from the tempest-tossed world—all the while, drawing on the social worlds of those past ages to continue to silence women, GLBTQ+ persons, and entire colonized cultures. Those marginalized people and communities are welcome to be part of the church but at the price of their silence and their obedience. No wonder Caputo dreams of "theologians to-come" who will be capable of risking the kind of danger and action that radical theology requires. Because the intellectual dishonesty of confessional theologians encourages further dishonesty in their communities, that dishonesty enacts the systemic sin of conventional self-protection—the kind of ideological closure that is utterly counter to that opening capacity of being called. All too often, the church is already aligned with a world closed inward in fear, striking out in self-protection, and profoundly detached from the ongoing reality and call of the world's suffering.

As we move on, it is important to see how Caputo's construction of sin, of hard-heartedness that is closed-in on itself—not just personally but corporately—interacts with Caputo's interpretation of that first topic as a profound capacity for, and openness to, difference in the midst of an uncertain world—a world that needs and calls for our risk. In these two moves we can already see that a proposal is underway, and that we are—in this proposal—being called to respond.

PROPOSED SOLUTION—THIRD MOVE

Precisely because the real "sin," or, the real problem that Caputo's proposal identifies in *Insistence* is the classical two-worlds theology still embedded in most confessional Christian traditions, Caputo's approach to the topic of Christology, is an approach suitable for a single-plane realism that is itself epistemologically uncertain all-the-way down. In his contribution to the 2018 book *Theology in the Age of Trump*, Caputo turned to Martin Luther King Jr.'s "Dream speech" on the Washington Mall in 1963, contrasting it with Donald Trump's claims to make America "great again."

> America is not only a geopolitical entity but an idea, a prayer, a dream—the one [M.L.] King spoke of when he said that the civil rights movement was "a dream deeply rooted in the American dream," in which all of God's people will be free, where freedom will ring from every mountain side. Then, and only then, King said, "will America be a great nation." Great, not with the power of an army but with what Joseph Nye calls the "soft power" of an

idea that lifts up the powerless, first not in military and economic force, but because there the first are last and the last are first.[26]

"America" concluded Caputo, in Derridean terms, "insists; it does not exist. Its existence is up to us."[27] Likewise, "God" insists; whether "God" exists—whether God becomes incarnate—is up to us.

Traditionally, in this third move of a proposal, classical and confessional Christian theologies claim that in the Incarnate Word, God has drawn near to humanity. In the singular, unique figure of Jesus, the Christ, who alone is the meeting place of the eternal and the temporal, God acts to save human beings from the sin of pride and disobedience through Jesus' humble and obedient death on the cross (Phil 2:6–11)—re-opening the possibility of human relationship with God, including the possibility of eternal life. Caputo sees this nostalgic worldview, with its absolute claims, to be the problem in need of a solution.

In contrast to the two-worlds' logic (i.e. eternal/temporal; divine/human) of classical and confessional theologies, Caputo's theology of perhaps, once again, moves theology out of the ontological business of *being*, and into the luring, calling, poetic, business. Key to his proposed poetics is a *chiasmic* (intertwining) structure of call and response that we have already seen at work in his core theme of hospitality. Now, in this third topic, it is important to see how his intertwining structure of call and response plays off confessional theology's intertwining of the divinity and humanity of Christ.

In his discussion of *theopoetics,* Caputo extends the *chiasmic* structure of call and response to discuss the relation between "insistence" and "existence." While Caputo has used insistence to critique the confessional emphasis on the existence of "God," he now turns to explaining the positive relation between insistence and existence. Like the structure of "call" and "response," the *insistence* of "God" seeks out human response. "God" comes to *exist*, however, argues Caputo, only insofar as humans decide to act on the inviting/troubling call of the event—courageously reaching out of themselves and beyond their secured interests. Thus, "God, perhaps" becomes "incarnate," not as a once-only event in a two-worlds logic of an eternal presence becoming human, but in ordinary life as human beings risk generosity and hospitality, breaking open the boundaries imposed by conventions, theological, political, gendered, class, and racial. To be clear, it is not the second person of the Trinity that becomes "real" in Caputo's model but the call that becomes realized by being acted upon.

---

26. Caputo, "The Time of America," 80.
27. Caputo, "The Time of America," 81.

In this proposal of "perhaps," people are not asked to believe in the doctrine of the incarnation, but to risk something, to do something that brings about the incarnation of a transformed life. Mary's yes to the call of the angel becomes democratized, as it were, our "yes" to the call, not only in word but in action that makes "God" real.[28]

> The name (of) "God" is not the subject of a set of representational truths about facts of the matter, which is what became of it in modernity. It comes in the form of stories and fables, sayings and parables, greetings and farewell. It is not verified but witnessed. The name (of) "God" is the name of a deed, not of an entity . . . The truth of the name (of) "God" takes the form of something to be done not of a proposition to be debated . . .[29]

This "weakness of God must be addressed by the strength of a response, which is its chiasmic partner. God needs us as much as we need God."[30] In utter contrast to the doctrinal position of God's aseity, therefore, Caputo underscores the way that "God,"—as in the story of the loud knocking in the middle of the night—needs our response to become real.

In contrast to the "logic" of strong, confessional theologies, a poetics, writes Caputo:

> is not an ornamentation, a decoration, but thinking that tries to put itself (*stellen*) forth (*vor*) in a discursive formation, or rather to put forth an event, to formulate an image, a picture, a story, a body of tropes that gives word to the event, to provide insistence with a discursive existence. It takes up the lived experiential intertwining, the *chiasm*, of life and world, . . . of the "life-world," of the sphere of life . . .[31]

Caputo affirms the importance of "thinking" in this passage, even as he insists on its being an evocative and provocative kind of thinking, like the parables that lure us away from abstract thought and into lived experience. By risking "to formulate an image, a picture, a story," etc., one "provides insistence with a discursive existence." This is to say, one seeks to bring the insistence of the event rhetorically to life, and this includes language about God.

In this third topic of a dramatically reimagined Christology we see Caputo reaffirming the goodness discussed in topic one as well as responding

---

28. See Luke 1:38.
29. Caputo, *Insistence of God*, 178–79; see also Caputo, *Weakness of God*, 116.
30. Caputo, *Insistence of God*, 116.
31. Caputo, *Insistence of God*, 115 (emphasis added).

courageously to the profound problem of human sin caught in narcissistic self-absorption—including in the spaces of church and the discourse of theology. We see in this Christology an attempt to open a genuinely new space personally but also politically that requires real courage. In this reimagined Christology, it becomes apparent that the audience—in its affirmation or denial of the message of Jesus—completes, or not, the action called for by Jesus' preaching of the Empire of God. Here it becomes apparent that Caputo wants his interpretations of these topics to be taken seriously. He desires and hopes that his hearers might experience a call in and through their engagement with the text and respond with a Yes! Yes!, as Caputo likes to say. A "yes" that will move into action.

Again, for both Farrell and Caputo, the audience completes the act of communication, not the speaker. But for listeners to act on that proposal they need to be seized or persuaded by it, which means that the speaker must also always be listening to them. To the extent that the interaction of these five topics creates a proposal that calls for and depends upon an active response, that textual interaction is a dynamic, rhetorical one.

While reminding readers of the importance of uncertainty that is present in all human acts of interpretation, Caputo's voice is neither neutral nor objective. Instead, his voice is guided by a listening that "attunes" itself intently, and passionately to the call that lies at the heart (*kardia*) of the "call and response" dynamic. Caputo's ears cling to that call, which calls its hearers to stand with and act on behalf of those at the margins, just as Jesus did in his preaching of the Empire of God.

THE NEW UN-GATHERED AND COSMIC COMMUNITY—FOURTH MOVE

Caputo's shift to a single-plane focus, in all its materiality, brings with it a very different view of human, and indeed, cosmic gathering. If in traditional confessional theologies, the Church is called into being by the Holy Spirit, who, through grace, inspires faith-as-right-belief, and leads human souls from this world to eternal life with God, Caputo's *theopoetics* envisions very different spaces and practices. As we saw in our discussion of the second move, namely how strong, confessional theologies seek out social and political power, Caputo's treatment of this fourth topic, following upon his democratic vision of Christology, insists on opening up our doctrinally closed habits when reflecting on the topic of the church.

Caputo sees in the scene of Matthew 25:31–46, persons who responded to others in real need without any sense of reward, and who lived out the radical economy of Derrida's language of the Gift. While Matthew, or a later redactor, turned the story into one of eternal rewards and punishments, what Caputo calls our attention to in the poetics of the story is a continuing call to open our lives, risking ourselves for others. That shift in interpretation generates a very different, much more open-ended proposal of authentic community.

Going back to his distinction between existence and insistence, Caputo acknowledges that confessional theology "is more or less the only theology that *exists* because it addresses the only kind of 'religion' that *exists*, the concrete confessional or historical traditions of religious beliefs and practices." He continues: "Kierkegaard described this in wonderfully polemical terms as the religion that comes replete with 'a full staff of bishops, deans, pastors,' with 'a complete inventory of churches, bells, organs, offering boxes, collection boxes, hymn boards, hearses, etc.' That is what exists."[32] Confessional theologians represent the strong theology of doctrinal truth and ritual correctness. Radical theology, by contrast, and in a way similar to Derrida's Justice, does not exist.[33]

> It [radical theology] has no national headquarters, holds no council, has no dogmas, takes up no collections, neither ordains nor excommunicates, and sends out no missionaries to knock on doors . . . Taking up no earthly room, existing in or as no earthly institution, it acts somewhat more like a hovering spirit that haunts the living confessional traditions, as a ghost that spooks their closed confessional assemblies, a specter that insists in what exists, insisting on being heard.[34]

Picking up especially on that last line's emphasis that radical theology "insists in what exists," Caputo argues that radical theology is "parasitic" upon confessional theologies, attempting to "question," "haunt," and "spook" their claims to truth, via the uncertainty of "one small word, 'perhaps.'" We, as readers, are now in a better position to see the parasitic character of weak theology on strong, confessional theologies. While Caputo cannot force readers to change their minds and hearts, he can "haunt" them, even as he holds out hope for the future. "Perhaps a thinking to come will be more willingly haunted, more ready for anxiety, more easily exposed to the disturbing specter of a certain groundlessness, of a certain uncertainty that gives life its intensity."[35]

32. Caputo, *Insistence of God*, 76 (emphasis added).
33. For Derrida on Justice, see below.
34. Caputo, *Insistence of God*, 76.
35. Caputo, *Insistence of God*, 82.

Throughout *Insistence*, Caputo offers Martha—from the story of Martha and Mary in Luke's gospel (10:38–42)—as a model of faith, describing her as a "postmodern host."[36] Playing off Meister Eckhart's allegorical interpretation of the story, Caputo agrees with Eckhart's preference for Martha's hospitality over Mary's devotion. In the Middle Ages, Jesus' approval of Mary's choice was seen as affirming the contemplative life over the more active life of service. Eckhart, by contrast, found in Jesus' words of response to Martha, "Martha, Martha," a "double gift." Martha was not only listening to Jesus but also doing the gospel, attending to Jesus' bodily, animal needs. In Eckhart's preference for Martha, Caputo finds the enactment of his understanding of faith, not as belief that buys into the two-worlds logic of classical theology, but as a response that acts.

> Martha knows that the insistence of God is not merely to be savored at the feet of Jesus, but urgently requires our assistance, the assistance that translates God's insistence into existence . . . There is realism and materialism in Martha that is missing from Mary's beautiful immaterialism that is never made real, and Jesus secretly prefers her [Martha's] materialism.[37]

By offering, along with Eckhart, the New Testament figure of Martha as a model of faith who responds to Jesus and his bodily needs, Caputo hopes to catch the imagination of confessional traditions. In so doing, he hopes to move them towards living out the *theopoetics* of call and response out of concern for the materiality of this world, and for the worldly, materiality of the human condition. Faith is about this life, and the "love of this life."[38]

Having seen Caputo argue that radical theology, like the weak force of justice, or "God," does not exist but haunts the lived existence of confessional theologies, it comes as no surprise that he is not interested, in *Insistence*, in developing any kind of Radical Theology Church. While the notion of "gathering," according to Caputo, is itself good, he invokes Derrida, who insisted that "dis-juncture, the opening," is better. The opening up of confessional theology is better than the gathering-in of another official community—holding to the prophetic priority of "the gap God *makes* not the gap God *closes* by gathering things together."[39] Thus, Caputo cautions against the rush to gather together and to speak of a renewed community precisely because that language tends toward a new lock-down or closure of allowable discourse.

---

36. See Luke 10:38–42.
37. Caputo, *Insistence of God*, 42.
38. Caputo, *Insistence of God*, 237.
39. Caputo, *Insistence of God*, 115.

Still, while Caputo has not leveraged his critique of confessional theology for any kind of institutional plan—no new dogma, no church fees, etc., that does not mean he does not desire something. He longs for those confessional theologians—in those "midnight moments" of "tossing and turning"—to be moved by the "haunting thought that what they call a gift of grace is an accident of birth—that had they been born in another time and place they would have entirely different things inside their heads than the things they defend in their daytime theologies."[40]

By haunting those confessional theologians with the radical contingency of their doctrinal truth claims, there remains hope that these confessional communities will become more open, more radicalized, turning their understanding of faith towards the poetic, *chiasmic* model of a lived response to the call. "My ultimate subject matter," says Caputo, "might be more properly described as the becoming-radical of confessional theology."[41] There is, then, a kind of conversion, of persuasion, at play here. Following Derrida, Caputo calls for a shift from "confession" of faith (*croyance*) as belief to "circumfession." "That radical confession [of the contingency of their lives and faith commitments] is what I mean by confessional theologians becoming circum-fessional, in which the accent switches from *confessio* as professing a creed to *confessio* as confessing how deeply exposed to events we are."[42]

Recognizing our vulnerability to events, Caputo suggests that the work of radical theology will continue to be that of exposing communities to the call for change and for justice.

> The 'cultural' and 'ethico-political' momentum of postmodern thinking is constituted by a gradually diffusive, disseminative, de-colonializing, and democratizing movement from men to women and children, from west to east, from north to south, from strong to weak—these are all genial features of 'weakness' for me—extending to everyone in any way marginalized in the old order, to 'the least among you' (Matt. 25:45).[43]

If the thrust of Caputo's *theopoetics* has emphasized the way the event—what's going on in the name (of) "God"—calls for a response, for the doing of the truth, within the human community, in the final portion of *Insistence*, Caputo argues for a yet more primal, more immediate sphere of belonging than he has explicitly considered thus far. Even as he broaches the subject of this wider sphere, he suggests that the focus of his *theopoetics* has been,

---

40. Caputo, *Insistence of God*, 72.
41. Caputo, *Insistence of God*, 61.
42. Caputo, *Insistence of God*, 72
43. Caputo, *Insistence*, 173.

perhaps, too intimate, too private. In the shift he now proposes from *theopoetics* to *cosmopoetics* he seeks to heal the tendency toward binary construction—not only of the human and the non-human, but of spirit and flesh.

By situating the *theopoetic* within the discourse of *cosmopoetics*, Caputo helps his readers move towards affirming the emergence of the *theopoetic*—evident in the broad variety of religious discourses including Christianity—*within* the yet more vast play of the universe. Challenging the traditional dichotomy of the human/non-human world, Caputo forcefully reminds readers that we are animals and that we belong to the earth, to the heavens, and to matter. "Perhaps, the human and the non-human are not opposites but intertwined," he writes. "Perhaps the *chiasm* (of call and response) obtains not only between God and human beings but between the human and the non-human."[44]

That we are "called upon or laid claim to by forces of a wider scope," means that we exist in this wider material world more deeply than we have ever let ourselves acknowledge. Forget the binary of "subject/object" by which we have long separated ourselves from nature. Instead, says Caputo, "We *are* the relation between our bodies and our world . . . we do not have to 'build a bridge' to the world. We are that bridge." Continuing with this materialist theme, he adds: "We are plants, sprouts shooting up from the local conditions in which we have been produced, in just the way that vegetation started to shoot up when the ozone layer grew thick enough to shield the earth from the ultraviolet rays of the sun . . ."[45] In this "religious materialism,"[46] care of and for the world, is an insistent natural call to which we can and must respond. Thinking of climate change, here, our destinies are inextricably linked.

I include here this expansion of his *chiasm* of call and response to the material world, precisely because Caputo is arguing that our relation to matter is more primal, more fundamental, than our traditional speech about what's going on in the topic of humanity created in the 'Image of God.' The real "church," as it were, the real sacred space opened up by Caputo's radical theology is not *contained* by *theopoetics* but by the opening of *theopoetics* onto *cosmopoetics*. If Paul could write in 2 Cor 5:17 "if anyone is in Christ there is a new creation," radical theology opens onto a more profound reimagination of that "new creation." In fact, for Caputo's radical theology, what we have seen is that the reimagined topic/move of "God" in the *chisam* of call and response (in which we come to see that "God" needs us as much

---

44. Caputo, *Insistence of God*, 171.
45. Caputo, *Insistence of God*, 176.
46. Caputo, *Insistence of God*, 170.

as we need "God"), is itself now situated in the horizon of the cosmos and its call. "*Theopoetics*," argues Caputo, is a "regional discourse inside a larger cosmic setting."[47]

> The cosmic counterpart to the call that is being called in the name of God (*theopoetics*) is the call of the world (*cosmopoetics*). That call is the "promise of the world". . . within which the name of God assumes its place as but one of several calls. The name of God is a first name, but only one of many first names, albeit one of paradigmatic significance in *theo-poetics*. But *theopoetics* belongs within *cosmopoetis*.[48]

Religion, in its various forms and names, calls us to open our lives beyond the conventions that have shaped our communities and traditions to this point. What's going on in the name of "God," is precisely that call to say "Yes," to say, "Come," even at the risk of our lives. And that call itself—the *chiasm* of call and response that religion is—is itself not a ticket to beyond the universe but a ticket to the fuller appreciation of the universe of which religion itself is a part.

Caputo writes: "Thinkers like . . . Derrida (following a certain 'Martha') are urging us to keep the momentum going."[49] "A *cosmopoetics* embraces an ever wider intertwining of the human and the non-human, recognizes the broader reach of "insistence," meaning that we are called upon or laid claim to by forces of a wider scope and that we must brace ourselves for a wider and more welcoming hospitality, one worthy of our model, Martha."[50] Indeed, Caputo argues that the model of Martha—combining insistence with existence—must be given "a cosmic import." Martha, he writes, "appreciates the materiality and worldly reality of the call." The sense of animal and material belonging that Caputo sketches is itself quite poetic. I quote here at some length.

> The cosmos opened up by Copernicus collapses the distinction between 'heaven' and 'earth,' one of the most cherished distinctions religion knows. The earth is itself a heavenly body, one more heavenly body made up of stardust, as are our own bodies. We are already heavenly bodies . . . every body—everybody, everything—is a heavenly body. Heaven is overtaken by the heavens. Dust to dust, indeed, but it is all stellar dust. Our bodily flesh is woven of the flesh of the earth, even as the earth itself

---

47. Caputo, *Insistence of God*, 174.
48. Caputo, *Insistence of God*, 177.
49. Caputo, *Insistence of God*, 173.
50. Caputo, *Insistence of God*, 174 (emphasis added).

is the debris of stars, the outcome of innumerable cyclings and recyclings of stellar stuff, all so many rolls of the cosmic dice.[51]

Linking the language of "grace," the gift of this life, to "chance," to "blind chance," Caputo is in awe that we are here at all—a profound gift. He continues, addressing the reader:

> Rather than "subjects" and "objects," think of our life and intelligence as something like the inside of the outside of the same thing, where the universe opens up a window on itself in order to peer within or engage in a moment of reflection. Our promptings are the promptings of the universe in us. That means whatever calls, whatever addresses and solicits us, whatever is getting itself called in us, is a calling of the universe, a way the universe has found of making its feelings felt, making its wishes known locally, in us. We are like a place where the universe takes a kind of qualitative leap or crosses a threshold, and the stars start talking to themselves.[52]

Caputo brings his own poetic skill to the task of underscoring and making explicit what was implicit in his theopoetics, namely, that we must let go of the mythology that we humans are in a special, divinely ordered space, given unique access to the hidden supreme being of God outside the universe. No, our experiences of "what's going on in the name of God" occurs within the universe. The universe/the cosmos, which is pure gift (and therefore also trouble) transcends us and transcends our regional discourses of God. We are not, in our "subjectivity," superior to, or over against nature, over against mere material objects. Instead, our belonging to the universe, to the world of animals and of things is itself profound, calling us to a yet deeper sense of realism and humility. The intimacy of human and non-human, spirit and flesh are being interwoven in this inter-stellar conversation.

Even as Caputo wants to encourage this feeling of connection to the vast un-unified universe, and the possibility that the universe comes to expression in part, through us, he also urges us readers to consider that perhaps, even here, we are not alone or unique or superior. Other intelligent life forms, writes Caputo, may "have already happened, and are happening elsewhere, and will continue to happen in innumerable places throughout the universe, before, after, and otherwise than us!"[53] If one understands Caputo's discussion of *cosmopoetics* as a further, vast widening of the belonging

---

51. Caputo, *Insistence of God*, 175.
52. Caputo, *Insistence of God*, 175.
53. Caputo, *Insistence of God*, 175.

to which we are called, and for which we are responsible, one can yet better see from the vastness of the cosmos, the generosity and humility with which our varying religious and humanistic traditions ought to view and interact with one another. In the vastness of the perspective itself, there seems to be a call for awe, humility, hospitality, and respect.

THE GIFT OF LIFE, MEANING, AND ESCHATOLOGY—THE FIFTH MOVE

If Caputo's language of *cosmopoetics* radically expands the space, the scope, of his *ecclesiology*, it also opens a much broader and materialist framework for the discussion of his fifth move, on the future, or *eschatology*. The overlapping interconnection of these topics/moves is particularly dense. Here, in this fifth topic, Caputo contemplates not only the final, meaningful, weighty things of human life but the end of the cosmos itself and the meaning/meaninglessness that its ending holds for us.

Thrown into the world, as Heidegger put it, we do not see life coming, as it were; we did not choose it. Yet, we love life. Caputo comments:

> because life is precious beyond belief, and life is made more precious by the realization that life lasts but a moment, not only personally but cosmically, that there are long stretches of the universe devoid of life, long eons before life existed, and there will be even longer eons when life will be no more. That means that to be alive, here and now, is a gift, like a miracle, which is the lived truth of geo-centrism.[54]

It is worth attending to Caputo's opening words above, "life is precious beyond belief." "Belief," of course, for Caputo, especially doctrinal belief, takes us out of the world; the preciousness "of life," on the other hand, affirms the surpassing gift of attending to this life, this earth, this world. This affirmation opens a discussion of the meaning of life, in light of the insistence of God, and the insistence of life itself.

In classical, confessional theology, questions about the future, about the end of time—the topic of eschatology—involved the logic of two-worlds and the journey, if all went well, of the soul to eternal life with God. Questions about the end of time gave way in the mid-20th century to existentialist questions about the meaning of life. Caputo plays off both eschatological traditions, offering a kind of materialistic nihilism—which is to say that there is no grand summing up of meaning, no fullness to be explicated.

54. Caputo, *Insistence*, 237–38.

As he points out, many cosmologists suggest "the universe is headed for oblivion."[55] Without a two-worlds view of reality, one might argue that that possibility of oblivion suggests a kind of meaninglessness to human experience. But Caputo insists, no. What such cosmic death points out is the incredible gift that life is. "For us, the exceptional moment is the time of life as a whole, the time while there is still life at all, and the interim ethics, or better still, the interim poetics, it imposes is the poetics of life itself, the insistent call of life itself. So while the opportune moment is still available to us, let us say yes to life, *viens, oui, oui*."[56]

Playing again off the language of Meister Eckhart, Caputo argues that the preciousness of life does not need a why. "The meaning *in* life, not the meaning *of* it, is found at the point that each day is found to be a grace, an event of grace, the grace of the event. The grace of life is not a gift bestowed upon the world by a Superbeing, but in an emergent effect *on* the plane of the world."[57] Beyond all "commercial exchanges" of two-worlds theology, and religion, Caputo remains steadfastly committed to the "plane of the world." "The categories of radical theology are ultimately categories of grace, of the gift, of the gratuitousness of life, of the 'for nothing else,' the 'for nothing more' of life, and life is this life. Life is only a gift, and a gift is only a gift if it is 'without why.'"[58] Here again, Caputo is not trying to tie up life in a nice bow. Uncertainty holds, which is why life can be hell. He writes: "Once again, in a *theopoetics* of the event, the idea is not to get rid of *Vorstellungen* like "heaven" and "hell" but to interpret them properly, in terms of events, and return them to the hell we produce on earth for ourselves and even more so for others, and to the heavenly graces of life which is beatitude enough."[59]

Nor is this expanded *theopoetics* attempting to silence the language of prayer. Far from it. While Caputo rejects the intervening, answering God of confessional theology, he lifts up our prayers and our tears raised out of the midst of suffering as profound expressions of faith loving life and longing for more life. These experiences of grief and anguish are faithful to life, faithful to the risk of saying "come," and, thus, aspects, too, of transformational grace. And so, one continues to say "yes" to life, "yes" to difference, to all the trouble that calls us out of ourselves. And, so, here in this fifth topic we see Caputo's proposal rejecting all theologies that promise a get-out-of-life-free

---

55. Caputo, *Insistence of God*, 224.
56. Caputo, *Insistence of God*, 225.
57. Caputo, *Insistence* of God, 239.
58. Caputo, *Insistence of God*, 244.
59. Caputo, *Insistence of God*, 242.

card. No, Caputo's theopoetic realism calls us into life and into our capacity to engage the suffering of others, and of ourselves, with courage and with hope.

"GOD" AND THE LONGING FOR JUSTICE

In classical theology, and works of Christian systematic theology, the topic of "God" is typically the first topic to be discussed because, as the tradition teaches, "God" is the presence that authorizes and calls creation into being. "God" is the one who ultimately controls all things, and because of that, how one interprets the reality of "God" controls how one interprets all the other topics, which are subordinate to the topic of "God." The task of systematic theology has been the logical, orderly presentation of a fixed and true order of official teaching. Here, however, I situate the discussion of "God," *following* the development of Caputo's proposal.

For Caputo, "God," if there is such a thing, is not "situated" above or outside the world, but is, instead, located within the experience of the call, or, *within* the *theopoetic* moves of his proposal. Indeed, I have called attention to statements he makes about "God" *within*, as it were, his proposal. "God" is less a particular topic than the transformative lure, the transformative call at work throughout the five topics.

In Caputo's body of work, no one thinker is as important in shaping Caputo's understanding of "God" as a provocative lure, than contemporary philosopher, Jacques Derrida. We can get some sense of the closeness between Caputo and Derrida in this response by Derrida to a question on the topic of God posed at the 2001 conference on Augustine at Villanova University.

> We usually identify God with the almighty, that is, with absolute power. I'm trying now in seminars and in texts, by following a political thread, to deconstruct, so to speak, the onto-theological politics of sovereignty. God is supposed to be absolutely powerful in our tradition. I don't know if it is Christian or not. I'm trying to think of some unconditionality that would not be sovereign, that is, to deconstruct the theological heritage of the political in our society concept of sovereignty, without abandoning the unconditionality of gifts, of hospitality, and so on. That means that some unconditionality might be associated, not with power, but with weakness, with powerlessness.[60]

---

60. Derrida, "The Force of Law, 41.

The first time I read this passage, I was struck by the very similar sets of image clusters that we see at work in Caputo's proposal. By challenging the logic and tropes of power, certainty, and sovereignty that have held sway in philosophy and across Western culture for centuries, Derrida is pursuing, in Farrell's terms, a "distinctly rhetorical undertaking." His is not an ontological inquiry; instead, Derrida says he is "following a political thread." Besides the structural similarity which suggests a working closeness between the two, Derrida's lecture, entitled "The Force of Law" is pivotal for understanding the shape of Caputo's discussion of "God."

Delivered at the Cardoza Law School in Brooklyn, New York in 1990, Derrida takes up the tension between Law and Justice. He argues that Law is a strong power. It can bind and limit human freedom and punish those who violate it. It has real, institutional force in the cultural worlds we inhabit. Justice, by contrast, has no such strong, official, or authorizing power; it has only the weak force of a call. There are no fines or jail time for ignoring justice. Ideally, of course, law seeks justice, but because law is always encumbered by context and particular concerns of the moment, it is impossible for laws to be fully just. Justice is a lure, therefore, to the law at its best, an insistent invitation to better ourselves and our culture, even as we know of many laws that have sought to oppress and violate the well-being of others.

Commenting on the text of that lecture, Caputo adds that for Derrida, his critical notion of "deconstruction" involves "a negotiation undertaken between a conditioned name (e.g., law) and an unconditional event, (e.g., justice)."[61] Caputo explains: "To deconstruct the law is to hold the constructedness of the law plainly and constantly in view so as to subject the law to relentless analysis, revision, and repeal, to rewriting and judicial review, in the light of the unconditional demand of justice."[62] For his part, Caputo aligns that Law/Justice dynamic with his own project of subjecting the contractedness of institutional "Christianity" to the relentless, unconditional questioning of the key event, harbored within the name "Christianity," namely, Jesus' proclamation of the Empire of God.[63]

---

61. Caputo, *Weakness of God*, 27. In *What Would Jesus Deconstruct?*, Caputo offers this reflection as well: "Deconstruction 'itself'—I do not actually think there is any such thing—is not a determinate position, a definite 'what' or worldview with a manifesto, or a platform or set of positions, theistic or atheistic, but a 'how,' a way of holding a position, of being under way or being on a path. It is an affirmation without being a self-certain and positive position. It does not occupy a position of opposition to Christianity or to any other concrete or determinate belief or practice. Deconstruction is rather more of a ghost, adding a specter to the Spirit whose lead we are trying to follow." 55.

62. Caputo, *Weakness of God*, 27.

63. Caputo, *Weakness of God*, 128–32.

Just as, according to Derrida, "deconstruction is justice,[64]" insofar as it continuously breaks open the conventionality and power structures of the present, Caputo argues, as we have seen, that theology should be doing something very similar, enacting a *theopoetics* of the kingdom, that corrects for Christian theology's overemphasis upon *logos* and static models of reason.

Derrida's Law/Justice dynamic does not *control* Caputo's proposal but *illuminates* it. The movement of strong theology to weak theology is analogous to the movement, never guaranteed or fixed, of Law towards Justice. Weak theology, for Caputo, is not a fixed formula; instead like Justice, it continues to interrupt, to summon, to draw the various constructions of strong theology out of themselves and out of their own defensive claims to certainty. It seeks to do on the page what it imagines the activity of "God, perhaps" is like.

---

64. Caputo, *Weakness of God*, 28.

7

Disrupting the Play of Hermeneutics

Caputo, as we have seen, is clearly concerned about the inclination of argumentation, debate, and even the language of proposals to be aligned with the language of "right belief," which is to say, embedded in metaphysical assumptions and static models of Truth. But, just as Caputo suggests that Derrida was overly influenced by a more traditional understanding of hermeneutics, I am inclined to say the same of Caputo's understanding of rhetoric.[1] He sees it through the lens of ornamentation, of dressing up what has already been decided, rather than as a public mode of invention. But, what of an approach to rhetoric that explicitly lays aside modern assumptions about autonomy, agency, and objectivity? What of an approach informed by the postmodern works of Derrida and Lévinas, among others, in the way that Caputo himself was moved beyond modern philosophy by such figures?

Much like deconstructionists, who, Caputo says, have gotten a "bad rap," these new rhetoricians find themselves dismissed as the "new sophists." Might such a new rhetoric fit with Caputo's effort to open up a new, slightly mad, sophistry, that would turn modernist assumptions of individuality, authority, and power on their head? I turn now to the work of rhetorical theorist, Diane Davis, and her book *Inessential Solidarity: Rhetoric and Foreigner Relations*, in which she articulates the importance of a revised rhetoric as

---

1. See Caputo, *Hermeneutics*, 191–215.

"First Philosophy."[2] Her approach to rhetoric, accounts as well for Caputo's rich language of call and response and his success in moving readers not only to tears, but to the danger and risk of exposing themselves to the leap of faith, to a doing that listens to the call in what Jesus called the Kingdom, or the Empire, of God. Along the way, I will show not only how Caputo's proposal already overlaps with hers but also where Davis rightly speaks of the call itself as a distinctly rhetorical phenomenon.

While Davis affirms the basic understanding of the interplay between rhetoric and hermeneutics as a mutual dependence upon one another, as discussed by Stephen Mailloux, she holds out for a "*non*-hermeneutical dimension of rhetoric that has nothing to do with meaning making, with offering up significations to comprehension."[3] Instead, and informed by the work of Lévinas, she writes:

> Preceding and exceeding all hermeneutic interpretation, it [i.e., the *non*-hermeneutical dimension] deals not in signified meaning but in the address itself, in the exposure to the other; it deals not in the 'said' (*le dit*) but in the 'saying' (*le dire*). The said indicates the constative production of conceptual forms, themes, ideas; it thus offers itself up to interpretation. The saying, by contrast, indicates a performative address that necessarily unsettles what is congealed in the already-said—most specifically for our purposes, it shatters the conceptual image that 'I' have interiorized of 'you,' which takes us both out, 'essentially.'[4]

Davis aligns the said—the "constative production of conceptual forms," etc., with hermeneutics, and saying with the interruptive priority of rhetoric. "There is no said without the saying, no hermeneutic understanding without this address which, in obligating me to respond, holds me in relation with an unassimilable other, exposing me to my irreparable exposedness, my radical non-selfsufficiency."[5]

Davis' discussion of Lévinas' saying aligns well with Caputo's discussion of the call—an event that befalls and overtakes us, shattering our actual worldview.[6] But more particularly, it aligns well with Caputo's insistence that Jesus' preaching of the "Kingdom of God" is just such an interruptive call or address, which exhibits the saying dimension of discourse rather than the

---

2. Davis, *Inessential Solidarity*, 14.

3. For a brief discussion of Steven Mailloux's work on "rhetorical hermeneutics," see Appendix I

4. Davis, "Addressing Alterity: Rhetoric, Hermeneutics," 192–93.

5. Davis, *Inessential Solidarity*, 84.

6. Davis, *Inessential Solidarity*, 11.

said.[7] Davis further aligns this non-hermeneutical dimension of rhetoric, to what she calls, quoting Lévinas, a "preoriginary" calling that binds us to the other. To elucidate this calling, she turns to Lévinas' famous discussion of the term face.

> For him [Lévinas], the "face" connotes neither the front of the head in a literal sense nor the effect of routine figural operations. Face, in Lévinas, has nothing to do with the color of the eyes or the shape of the lips or the size of the ears, or how much the other resembles, say, the mother—according to him, as long as you are attuned to any of this, you are not encountering a face.

She continues:

> Neither visible nor conceivable nor perceivable, face "is what cannot become content, which your thought would embrace; it is uncontainable, it leads you beyond" (EI, 87). What one encounters in the face to face *is* the other's finitude, the other's exposedness—that is to say, both his or her mortality (susceptibility to wounding, to ravaging illness, to "the cold and the heat of the seasons") and, simultaneously, his or her transcendence as sheer ungraspableness. (OTB, 91)[8]

For Lévinas, writes Davis, the face "speaks". . . "The relation with the face is already a language relation, a saying or an address." In fact, "in the 'face' of the other, 'I' am . . . under an intractable obligation to respond, an ethico-rhetorical responsibility to respond."[9] Forget the notion of any authoritative "I" here; there is no individual autonomy. "According to him," writes Davis, "the existent (the 'subject') emerges . . . only in *response* to alterity and therefore exists for-the-other (nonindifference) before it ever gets the chance to exist for-itself (indifference)."[10]

We are born *host-ages*, according to Lévinas—called, obligated, to a "solidarity," as Davis puts it, to respond to the other (not only the already "Same," like "us"), and not from the starting point of our already autonomous voice, but from the acknowledgment that there is no self prior to the call of the other.[11] There is no self, no sure-footed, grounded philosophy, no individual grasping the unity of all things prior to the call of rhetoric.

---

7. Caputo, *Weakness of God*, 277–78.
8. Davis, *Inessential Solidarity*, 11–12.
9. Davis, *Inessential Solidarity*, 12.
10. Davis, *Inessential Solidarity*, 14.
11. Davis, *Inessential Solidarity*, 14.

The preoriginary call, for which Lévinas uses the image of the face, insists not only on a capacity to respond but an obligation to respond. Davis writes: "in the encounter with the face, 'it is necessary to speak of something,' 'of the rain and fine weather,' of anything at all, 'but to speak, to respond to him (sic) and already to answer for him'" (sic)[12] There is, in the encounter with the face, an embodied responsibility to speak, to write, to publish, to get public, to risk one's own, ever-emerging voice in response to the provocation of the other.

What begins with the most trivial of invitations—to speak of the "fine weather"—is already an invitation to much deeper waters of commitment. And, just so, Caputo's proposals in *Against Ethics*, in *Weakness*, and *Insistence* begin with a rhetoric of invitation, relying on a potency, a capacity and obligation to respond in a way that will move beyond the opening call. These proposals move us to move on and move out, exposing us to our exposedness, and calling us to obligation, and from thence, for Caputo at least, to the possibility, beyond ethics, to faith, to confession and the practice of a new *Lebensraum*. As Davis, commenting on Lévinas writes: "(In) the beginning (my beginning, my *archē*) was the response . . . This positing necessarily grants a 'sense of 'oneself' but only as an *effect* of response-ability, as an 'accusative that derives from no nominative (OTB,11). What Lévinas is proposing is that a responsibility to respond, a preoriginary rhetorical imperative, is the condition for any conscious subject rather than the other way around."[13] Davis goes on to highlight a late essay by Lévinas, "Everyday Language and Rhetoric Without Eloquence." In it, "[r]hetoric," he says, "is what *gives* 'objects' to be seen and thought: thought does not begin with 'the reception of a datum by perception,' . . . but with the 'language that has formed it.' "But," she continues, "more important for our purposes, he [Lévinas] acknowledges that the saying itself names a kind of rhetorical gesture, an address that approaches the other directly, with neither agenda nor eloquence."[14] . . ."The *said* of any saying may be 'eloquent' or 'truly moving.' But the saying itself interrupts the semantic power of the trope, opening a relation with nonappropriable otherness."[15] In this initiating gesture or appeal, Davis sees a rhetorical act, prior to all symbolization, that opens onto and calls for interpretation, but more than this, calls for action—obliging us to respond.

12. Davis, *Inessential Solidarity*, 12.
13. Davis, *Inessential Solidarity*, 105–6.
14. Davis, "Addressing Alterity," 209.
15. Davis, "Addressing Alterity," 210.

"Forget ontology, epistemology—even ethics," Davis writes. "What Lévinas shows us without seeing is that rhetoric is first philosophy."[16] And perhaps, I might add, "first theology," as well. For what Caputo, "shows us without seeing" is the rhetoric of the preoriginary call that calls us always already with the call of something to do. Davis writes: "Being and knowing surely do follow, but if it were not for the irremissible inclination, this preoriginary obligation to respond, then in the face of the other I would nonchalantly file my nails. The face comes through each time as pure appeal, persuasion without a rhetorician..."

> The face teaches me an exorbitant responsibility without limits or final payoffs: 'The debt increases in the measures that it is paid,' Lévinas writes (OTB, 12). Yet if it were not for this preorginary obligation, the 'unconditionality of being hostage,' Lévinas tells us, there would be no generosity in the world—no compassion, no pardon, no proximity, 'even the little that there is' (OTB, 117). The priority of the other is 'presupposed in all human relationships,' Lévinas writes. And if that were not the case, 'we would not even say, before an open door, 'After you, sir!"' (sic)[17]

For Lévinas, the "face" corresponds to the "saying," to which we are always already called to respond.

In another discussion of the saying and the said, Davis comments on how Lévinas saw not only the importance of the event, the ungraspable saying becoming named, but also of the already named said (think of tradition and Scripture) sharing in the disruptiveness of the saying, the breaking open of the present.

Lévinas acknowledges that it is necessary that "the saying... be thematized, that it manifest itself, that it enter into a position and a book." But he goes on to argue that the "reduction" of the said to the saying is also necessary; indeed, he insists that it is the task of philosophy to not allow "what is beyond essence" to "congeal into essence."[18] Caputo, I believe, would agree as he writes on the reduction/transformation of the said to the saying: "The event harbored in these names [such as God] must not be trapped inside them. Accordingly, I want to impede the closure of these names, to block their literalization or ontologization... [S]acredness not only tolerates but demands deliteralization, and this in virtue of the event they shelter."[19] Davis'

---

16. Davis, *Inessential Solidarity*, 14.
17. Davis, *Inessential Solidarity*, 14–15.
18. Davis, *Inessential Solidarity*, 16–17.
19. Caputo, *Weakness of God*, 4.

description of the saying aligns well with Caputo's discussion of the call as an event that befalls and overtakes us, shattering our actual worldview[20]—as well as Caputo's insistence that the "kingdom of God" in Jesus' preaching is such an interruptive call or address, and thus exhibits the saying dimension of discourse rather than the said.

In a section of *Weakness* entitled, "Reduction of the Name of God," Caputo describes the impossible task of naming definitively or finally "the event that is astir in this name [God]." He writes: "The name of God is the name of what is called for in the kingdom . . . But this name, and the event that is astir in this name, is like the name of every event exposed to endless translatability, into other names of comparable excess, other names with comparably bottomless or overreaching powers of surprise and solicitation."[21] In the language of Lévinas, what Caputo describes here is a reduction from the saying (*le dire*) of the event into the said (*le dit*) of the name, "God," which itself remains open to "endless translatability." But then there is, in *Weakness*, a second reduction titled "Reduction of the Word of God." Here, Caputo says, the "Word of God, the Scriptures" undergoes what he calls a methodological transformation into an event.[22]

In Lévinas's terminology, one moves from the said of the text to the saying of the event experienced by the reader/hearer in the encounter with the said. Similarly, in Caputo's hermeneutical phenomenology, one no longer reads the Scriptures as either the object of historical-critical study, or as the divinely inspired, literal Word of God, but instead as a possible event. "For these texts are solicitations that call for a response, appeals coming from I know not where about a way to be, a style of existence, about a poetic possibility that we are invited to transform into existential actuality."[23]

Turning to a discussion of method in her own book, Davis states that the "primary method," for her text, *Inessential Solidarity*, involves a "cautious figuring of the unfigurable, a reduction of the saying to the said." She writes: "I've been attempting to trope that which no figure can contain, to mediate a trace of the immediate, to attend to the unthematizable by necessarily and simultaneously thematizing it." But there is another way, and Davis suggests she is more drawn to it. "The secondary method which is perhaps less familiar . . . involves a kind of reversal or rewinding—the reduction of the said to the saying. In Lévinas' words, this approach attempts 'to awaken in the said

---

20. For one of many passages in *Weakness* on this theme, see p. 11.
21. Caputo, *Weakness of God*, 115, 118–19.
22. Caputo, *Weakness of God*, 117.
23. Caputo, *Weakness of God*, 16 (emphasis added).

the saying which is absorbed in it.' (OTB 43). It attempts, that is, to allow the saying to show itself within the said by performatively interrupting it."[24]

It is that call, and that event, that fixes Caputo's attention in his reading of the Scriptures. "The eyes, or rather the ears, of this poetics are firmly fixed on the call, on the way of life that is called for, on the event of the kingdom, the style of the rule of God, that is embedded in these sayings and stories (in Scripture). The ears of this poetics are finely cocked to hear the call that emanates from them, to respond to the weak force of their strong appeal."[25]

Davis, for her part, also writes of being similarly, yet differently, attuned. "My receptors are rhetorically tuned, so in this case the charge that announced itself to me was not only to expose exposedness ... but to demonstrate that the exposure to exposedness issues a rhetorical imperative, an obligation to respond that is the condition for symbolic exchange."[26] It is this "underivable" (or, as Caputo would say, "from we know not where") "rhetorical imperative," a call always already in language, that calls for interpretation and action, which reveals the tension in the work of writing and reading. Davis comments: "This exposition takes place in writing and through writing—broadly speaking, 'writing' as any performance of the [preorginary] inscription, aural, visual and so on—a sharing that testifies to the shattering limit by 'touching' it ... The exposition depends on a writing (a saying) that undermines and interrupts language's awesome powers of representation."[27]

Davis then writes, or perhaps 'confesses,' her own experience of being "on the receiving end" of that imperative, invoking not only Lévinas but Jean Luc Nancy. "Nancy's call 'to expose the unexposable' [e.g., in writing] came through to me as an assignment that I could not refuse—I did try for a while—an undeniable charge to which this present work attempts to respond." She continues: "The one who writes is first of all called upon to write, put 'on assignment,' ... so that one is always writing in response to the Other and because there are others. An encapsulated interiority would have no need or desire to write; writing, no matter what it says, testifies to exposedness, to vulnerability—to responsivity."[28]

Think of Caputo's language of being "called on the carpet," as well as his request, near the end of *Weakness*, for us readers to consider "that the

---

24. Davis, *Inessential Solidarity*, 16.
25. Caputo, *Weakness of God*, 121.
26. Davis, *Inessential Solidarity*, 9.
27. Davis, *Inessential Solidarity*, 8
28. Davis, *Inessential Solidarity*, 9.

present study be viewed as my *Confessions*."[29] His own sense of being on-call, and called to confession, rhymes with Davis' being "put on assignment," even as she writes, like Augustine! that she did "try for a while" to refuse to respond to that call. And in both that evasion and her eventual response we can hear Caputo's ultimate inability to set "truth" aside. He writes of it:

> Truth is less something I seek rather than something I cannot evade... In this sense a confession is less a profession than a concession. To confess the truth means to own up to our own limits, to face the music about what we know and do not know. That is why truth is always something we can walk away from, ignore, distort, or repress (it is a weak force and lacks an army).[30]

Just as Davis argues that she has located in Lévinas, a rhetorical connection that he himself failed to see, I believe her work helps readers, and perhaps Caputo as a reader of his own work, see how powerfully persuasive his work can be for an audience no longer moved by the authority of fixed truths.

What if we take Davis' proposal seriously? Does her treatment of Lévinas on the topic of "the face"—and her language of a "preoriginary obligation to respond"—ring true to Caputo's figure of a "call without a caller?" And could that preoriginary obligation, which always already orients us to the other, be what is "going on" in the name of "God?"—a call always already calling us, obligating us, to profound relation? Could Caputo's call without a caller be not simply poetic but rhetorical, shaping the urgency as well as the "partialist" character of the call?

---

29. Caputo, *Weakness of God*, 287.
30. Caputo, *Weakness of God*, 287.

8

Confession

Near the end of *The Weakness of God* Caputo asks *us*, his readers, to "[I]ndulge for a moment my authorial conceit that the present study is to be viewed as my *Confessions*."[1] By placing his own "weak" work within the gravitational pull of Augustine's autobiographical classic, Caputo claims a moment of privilege, inviting the reader to re-read his book in light of Augustine's, or, even more boldly, alongside it. His invocation of the term "literary conceit," is itself noteworthy. In a brief discussion of the term, creative writing instructor, Ian Matthews, says that the function of a literary conceit

> is to let the writer show the depth of their feelings about their subject. The feeling must be so deep and powerful that only this specific, extended, and elaborate comparison can truly show the reader how the writer feels. The more metaphors, juxtapositions, and similes the writer can use, the more convincing the comparison becomes. In this way, the conceit is almost an argument that the writer is proving to the reader. Each new comparison is a new piece of evidence to prove the writer's case for the overall comparison.[2]

Matthew's analysis points to the overlap of the poetical and the rhetorical—the literary conceit functioning as a felt moment of revelation, on the one

1. Caputo, *Weakness of God*, 287 (emphasis added).
2. Conceit in Literature: Concept & Examples | What is a Conceit?—Video & Lesson Transcript | Study.com.

hand—showing Caputo's depth of feeling, as he pours forth his tears in the surrounding passages, while also urging his readers, in a way "almost like an argument," to compare the rhetorical force of Augustine's prayers with his own, each placing their own experience of transformation, in conversation with a new, emerging worldview.

Addressing that prayerful orientation, Caputo reminds us, *his* readers, how Augustine staged, or positioned, himself in the text of his *Confessions*—facing away from the reader "as he stands or kneels, *coram Deo*" (before God). Caputo then claims this staging for himself.

He writes: "Like Augustine in the *Confessions*, I have all along been offering up an open confession for the benefit of all to see and hear."[3] He confesses, amidst his tears, how he has entered into the risk of sharing his private questions in public. And just as Augustine allowed his readers to overhear him, as it were, at prayer, allowing them to see his inner, private questions, his longings, tears, and desires, so Caputo invites his readers to be moved, not by anything as crass as an argument, but by his prayers and by his tears. Might *we* be moved to the point of coming along beside him, relinquishing our claims to power and authority, opening our hearts, to the possibility of a call that calls us to turn around (*metanoia*), in part by opening ourselves to what Caputo has himself shared?

Even as Caputo hopes that sharing his private experience of being *coram Deo*, before God in prayer, might move *us*, his readers, to experience that gift in our personal lives, he also hopes that we, his readers, might be persuaded by the "weakness of what he has to say" to reconsider the nature of theological discourse itself. He longs and hopes, in other words, that his writing might be a call that moves his audience not only to a new understanding and risk of doing the truth but to a new understanding of theology as *theopoetics*.[4]

Augustine, writing, in prayer, at the beginning of Book Eight of the *Confessions*, reveals not only his thanks to God but also his hopeful strategy for moving his readers to faith. "Lord, you have broken my bonds. I will narrate how you broke them asunder. And when they hear these things, let all who adore you say, 'Blessed be the Lord of heaven and earth.'"[5] Just so,

---

3. Caputo, *Weakness of God*, 285.

4. Augustine's *Confessions* is a profound work of rhetoric and hermeneutics of transformation. By locating his own text as a contemporary "*Confessions*," Caputo might hope that his readers may be as moved by his work as he has been by Augustine's. At another level, just as Augustine's *Confessions* was not merely his "personal story," but his own rhetorical shaping of Christian theology as informed by a Neoplatonic view of reality, Augustine's work cannot be described as only poetic but also as rhetorical.

5. Augustine, *Confessions*, trans. Ryan.

Caputo, in *Weakness,* longs not only that his individual readers be released, liberated from ontology, but also freed for public discourse, transformed, and called "to seek a newer world."[6]

Augustine's *Confessions* model for Caputo the sinching up, as it were, of the private and the public. Imagine: there is Augustine, not only in the experience of prayer before God but also sharing that personal intimacy as he writes the *Confessions.* He allows his readers to overhear, and perhaps join in, as they read his prayers and absorb the moving report of Augustine's tears. And he does so all in the hope that his story might move them, might illuminate the twists and turns of their stories, such that his story might become theirs, or authorize them to share as he has.

In *Weakness,* Caputo is "fessing up," confessing as a theologian, that the discourse of theology must be radically changed, must relinquish its claims of power—what he calls "strong" theology—to the point of embarrassing and profound, public weakness. And, here again, in a way similar to Augustine, Caputo longs that this public confession might, perhaps (always tentative, never certain) move his readers to open themselves to a *theopoetics* beyond belief.

It is not by chance that Caputo closes *Weakness* with a "Concluding Prayer" that is full of public tears, weeping, and longing, ending his work with a rhetorical *peroratio* in the grand style. Comments Compier on Cicero's grasp of the necessity of that style:

> Finally, the grandiloquent style pulls out all the stops of passion as it moves the hearers. In Cicero's mind every effective discourse had to avail itself of this grand style to some degree, for 'to sway is victory.' Without moving the emotions of the audience the orator cannot achieve persuasion.[7]

Similarly, for Caputo's own beloved, Augustine, it was rhetoric that was charged with addressing the ambiguity and hesitancy in human responsiveness. The great Christian rhetor, writes in *De doctrina christiana*:

> when something is to be done and he (sic) [the teacher] is speaking to those who ought to do it but do not wish to do it, then those great things should be spoken of in the grand manner, in a way appropriate to the persuasion of their minds."[8]

---

6. The phrase is Robert F. Kennedy's, from a speech given in South Africa on June 6, 1966. American Rhetoric: Robert F. Kennedy—University of Cape Town Day of Affirmation Address, accessed July 19, 2024.

7. Compier, *What Is Rhetorical Theology?* 7.

8. Augustine, *De doctrina christiana*, 145.

Among many possible passages I could use at this juncture, here is Caputo himself writing, in *Weakness*, about what it will take for the impossibility of the Empire of God to become actual, real, and true.

> When we call for the kingdom to come, therefore, we are being called upon to push against these [strong] limits, to strain against these conditions, to practice a mad and unconditional hospitality, which is impossible . . . We are pressed to put our own power at risk, our home and our community, to seek out the lame and lepers, outcasts and outsiders.[9]

In these passionate lines, we hear again, but now in Caputo's own words, a rhetorical enactment of that "grand style" that calls out heroic action in *us*, his readers. The acts that the above passage calls for: "straining against," "pushing against," practicing "mad hospitality"—are exorbitant images of pressure, of stress and strain, the acts of heroes, and voices of resistance pressuring the systems of the world to change.

Given the importance of Augustine's *Confessions* to Caputo, it is important to keep before us, as readers, that he clearly rejects Augustine's Christian Neo-Platonism, and Christianity's continued institutional clinging to that worldview fifteen hundred years later. Even as Augustine claimed to have put his rhetorical past behind him in his new embrace of Christian truth, while brilliantly using his autobiographical narrative to offer, enact, and perform on the page, a theological proposal informed by Platonic and Neo-Platonic philosophy, so Caputo rhetorically draws on the philosophical company of Derrida to great effect.

In contrast to Augustine's classical worldview of divine truth, expressed in doctrinal authority, and longing for eternal rest in a literal, eternal, castle-like heaven, Caputo's concluding words and prayers reach for something else going on under the name of God: not stability but disruption, unsettling the conventional claims of Christian tradition. For as Caputo daringly puts it, "God . . . brings not the tranquility of order, pace my dear Augustine, but the disturbed, disjointed disorder, the cracks in the surface of too much order through which the shoots of justice spring."[10]

---

9. Caputo, *Weakness of God*, 262–63.
10. Caputo, *Weakness of God*, 285.

Appendix I

Hearing Footsteps: A Brief Look at Poetics and Rhetoric in the Time of Caputo

P ROFESSIONAL DISCUSSIONS OF RHETORIC, poetics, and hermeneutics have been ongoing across Caputo's career. His focus on hermeneutics over against classical metaphysics and rhetoric was underwritten in significant part by attending to the works of Heidegger, Gadamer, Derrida, and Levinas, among others. Specifically, his critique of metaphysics and the ontologically laden language of "theory," underscores the uncertainty within which all language, and, hence, all human experience within language, exists. It is this philosophical recognition of uncertainty that fundamentally, for Caputo, re-contextualizes the work of theology, moving from modernity's confidence in the facticity of Being and the philosophy of enduring presence, to a post-modern humility uncertain of any such grounding, which opens up new possibilities for a theology that moves in the direction of poetic experimentation.

Caputo's emphasis on uncertainty rhymes with the work of scholars also interested in rhetoric. In a collection of 1989 essays, titled *From Metaphysics to Rhetoric*—a title suggested by Chaim Perelman—he [Perelman] opens the book by discussing the turn to uncertainty and the work of informal logic, including dialectic and rhetoric.[1] In the same volume, Paul Ricoeur's essay, "Rhetoric—Poetics—Hermeneutics," discusses the

1. Meyer, ed., *From Metaphysics to Rhetoric*.

important contributions of each of these discourses for the new, uncertain world of thought and action, along with the tendency of each to claim the entire field of discourse for itself, a concern shared by Derrida, certainly with respect to both rhetoric and hermeneutics.[2]

Rebecca Chopp's 2001 essay, "Theology and the Poetics of Testimony," plays off Ricoeur's combination of rhetoric, poetics, and hermeneutics, while also clarifying the distinction between rhetoric and poetics in her work.

> My use of "poetics" points toward a kind of writing that exists outside much of modern theory. Such discourse is an invention, for it must create language, forms, images to speak of what, in some way, has been ruled unspeakable or at least not valid or credible to modern reason. Compared to rhetoric, poetics seeks not so much to argue as to re-figure, to reimagine and refashion the world.[3]

Chopp's attempt to align rhetoric with arguing, while aligning poetics with "invention," seems a bit overdrawn. To what end, one might ask, does one wish to "re-figure, re-imagine, and re-fashion the world?" Are such re-figurings not offered within what Seamus Heaney calls the "gravitational pull" of the world?[4] Pressing on that question moves the discussion of poetics in a more rhetorical direction. Perhaps rhetoric has been reduced too often to argumentation, narrowly considered as a kind of applied logic, without adequate attention to rhetoric as a creative art and practice—an episodic art—emerging within the unpredictable flux of *events* as a response to a call that must be engaged, calling for courage in the face of a past that must be faced and a future one cannot see coming.

Concerning the inventional character of rhetoric, Farrell writes: "I now wish to suggest that rhetoric, despite its traditional and quite justifiable association with the preservation of cultural truisms, may also perform an act of critical interruption where the taken for granted practices of a culture are concerned."[5] In these lines Farrell suggests something akin to Caputo's sense of *repeating forward*, which involves interpreting a past text but "in a new way."[6]

---

2. See Derrida's conversation with Gary Olson about the problem of "rhetoricism."
3. Chopp, "Theology and the Poetics of Testimony," 61; emphasis added.
4. Heaney, "Crediting Poetry," 414.
5. Emphasis in text. See, Farrell, *Norms of Rhetorical Culture*, 111. "The discourse of the call also functions as a rhetorical interruption: it comes to us from something other than ourselves—Being, God, other people-something that speaks of the importance of authenticity, responsibility, and justice."
6. See, for example, Caputo's chapter, "Repetition and *Kinesis*: Kierkegaard and

Appendix I: Hearing Footsteps

George Lakoff's work, with Mark Johnson, called *Metaphors We Live By* (1980), but also his work with Mark Turner, *More than Cool Reason: A Field Guide to Poetic Metaphor* (1989), are important for this discussion. Key to Lakoff's body of work is the idea that there is no absolute objectivity, that ordinary, conventional reality, as we think of it, is metaphorically constituted.

> What the myths of objectivism and subjectivism both miss is the way we understand the world through our interactions with it. What objectivism misses is the fact that understanding, and therefore truth, is necessarily relative to our cultural conceptual system and that it cannot be framed in any absolute or neutral conceptual system. Objectivism also misses the fact that human conceptual systems are metaphorical in nature and involve an imaginative understanding of one kind of thing in terms of another.[7]

For its part, subjectivism "also misses the fact that metaphorical understanding involves metaphorical entailment, which is an imaginative form of rationality."[8]

While Lakoff speaks frequently of the importance of "understanding," his focus on the metaphorical character of language is directed to the rhetorical shaping of discourse to impact others. As I point out in the text, his work in *Moral Politics* parallels Caputo's desire for what Lakoff calls an "imaginative form of rationality." While Lakoff does not speak of "hermeneutics," per se, he does call attention to the way, in political discourse, that candidates and their campaigns utilize metaphors to actively shape the choices and decisions facing the voters.[9]

The notion of framing is important for Lakoff because it illuminates his rhetorical interest in how Democratic progressives might become as skillful as conservative Republicans in shaping what is culturally at stake in the issues and decisions facing the country. While Caputo speaks more from the language of obligation, of *being grasped*, his distinction between "strong" and "weak" theologies rooted, as it were, not in ontology but in the play

---

the Foundering of Metaphysics," in his book *Radical Hermeneutics*. And see, too, his discussion of "repetition" and "truth," in Caputo, *Truth* 86. "Repetition is the way the truth-event stays moving, its preferred mode of transportation. Repetition is the mode of moving forward, *repeating forward*, repeating what has been up to now but in a new way. Repetition *produces* what it repeats. . . . The result of repetition is something new and creative, for which the author must take responsibility . . ."

7. Lakoff and Johnson, *Metaphors We Live By*, 193–94.
8. Lakoff and Johnson, *Metaphors We Live By*, 194.
9. Parrott, "George Lakoff's New Happiness," 414.

of language, shares Lakoff's productive, constructive play of "strong father" and "nurturant parent." When I read Lakoff's comment that "conservatives hold a worldview centering on authority and competition," and that "empathy is at the center of the progressive moral worldview,"[10] I think of my chart in chapter one comparing the language of Strong and Weak theologies.

The following scholars, Stephen Mailloux and Michael C. Leff, have been determined to hold rhetoric and hermeneutics together, but with differing emphases. Australian scholar, Mailloux, took up the connection between hermeneutics and rhetoric in 1985. In line with Caputo's critique of "theory," and metaphysical reason, including practical reason, Mailloux, in his essay, "Rhetorical Hermeneutics," demonstrates the inadequacy of both "realist" and "idealist" conceptions of literary theory. He asks: "What happens when the theorist stops searching for that general account that guarantees correct readings? Where does he (sic) go once he (sic) quits asking realist or idealist questions about interpretation? One route to follow takes a turn toward rhetoric . . . I propose a rhetorical hermeneutics, an anti-Theory theory."[11]

Mailloux acknowledges the traditional awareness of the interplay between rhetoric and hermeneutics, namely that "[r]hetoric is based on interpretation and interpretation is communicated through rhetoric." In such a conception, hermeneutics involves the frame of reception, while rhetoric involves the frame of composition or production. But by itself, that traditional description fails to move beyond foundationalist arguments. A rhetorical hermeneutics, says Mailloux, can help philosophical and hermeneutical theorists avoid various forms of foundationalism and certainty. He writes:

> A rhetorical hermeneutics must, by necessity, be more therapeutic than constructive. To be otherwise, to construct a new account of interpretation in general, would simply reinvoke the same old problems of realism and idealism. Rather than proposing still another interpretive system on all fours with realist and idealist theories, rhetorical hermeneutics tries to cure theoretical discourse of its Theoretical tendencies.[12]

His position here—in contrast to the debates between "realism" and "idealism" which dominated much of mid-twentieth century literary theory—fits nicely with Caputo's project of radical hermeneutics that seeks not so much to get away from tradition but to heal it of its foundationalism—i.e., its tendencies toward the parallel problems of supernaturalism and naturalism, and

---

10. Lakoff, *Political Mind*, 60.
11. Mailloux, "Rhetorical Hermeneutics," 629.
12. Mailloux, "Rhetorical Hermeneutics," 630.

Appendix I: Hearing Footsteps

its quests for both certainty and power. Such insights rhyme as well with rhetorical theorists, like Farrell, who point to rhetoric as a public discourse that at once lies beyond theory and plays creatively with traditions—parasitically inventing, in dynamic interaction with audiences, new approaches to what he calls "social knowledge."[13] Nonetheless, while Caputo can acknowledge, on the fringes of his proposal, the importance of "persuasiveness," and can affirm, as well, the play of "rhetorical tropes," he, unlike Mailloux, tends to fold rhetorical invention into a more totalizing view of hermeneutics.

Leff's essay, "Hermeneutical Rhetoric," plays off Mailloux's work, reversing the terms "so that the stress falls on rhetoric." "The focal interest here centers on rhetorical practice as manifested in texts that directly and overtly engage political circumstances . . . To put the point simply: where Mailloux asks how rhetorical strategies enter into hermeneutical activity, I ask how hermeneutical strategy enters into the production of political rhetoric."[14] Leff goes on to produce a fascinating case study, showing how Abraham Lincoln's interpretation of the significance of the Declaration of Independence changed over time and across varying contexts, most importantly in the construction of his Gettysburg Address. Here, as with Mailloux, we see Leff demonstrating the interaction and interdependence of hermeneutics and rhetoric.

---

13. Farrell, *Norms of Rhetorical Culture*, 75–76.
14. Leff, "Hermeneutical Rhetoric," 309.

Appendix II

"Why Are These the Topics?"
A Political and Theological Response[1]

"Why are these the topics?" my friend asked, coming out of a theological lecture one fall afternoon when we were both students at the University of Chicago back in the 1980s. "Why are these the topics? Can't we ever be done with sin and grace, Christology and the Church? Can't we just move on?" And I found myself laughing then not only with her frustration but at the very real insight of the question. Why these topics indeed!

As I think of that conversation years ago, I am now ready to offer a response that I hope responds in a helpful way. The reason that variations on the themes or topics of (1) creation/image of God, (2) sin, (3) Christology, (4) the Church with its language of grace and faith, and (5) eschatology are the continuing topics of Christian theology is because they are the Christian *names* for the set of moves, which mark virtually any form of public proposal that invites persons into a cooperative venture. The topics of Christian theology are not, to put it bluntly, as utterly unique as Christian tradition might wish to have it. The topics emerge instead out of the fundamentally rhetorical nature of virtually any public situation in which a person or group is proposing that a community join to move together in a particular

---

1. Bessler, part of a longer essay, "Moving Words: The Political Life of Theology." For the text of the Clinton address: Clinton, "Democratic Presidential Nomination Acceptance Address."

direction. That proposed direction might be toward the vitality of the new in contrast to the deadening oppression of the old, or to the integrity of the old in contrast to the banality of the new. It might be a call to stay the course; it might be a call to change courses. It might be a call to listen to others more deeply but it could be a call to ignore others.

Proposals of leadership call us to move in various directions, but the formal elements of such diverse proposals remain fairly stable. When theologians engage those five topics, they do so not simply for the sake of argumentative coherence but because they are the topics by which theologians make proposals for how Christian faith communities should understand themselves and engage their world in time and place.

Because we are not used to thinking of theology in this way, I want to share another experience from nearly thirty years ago that began to change my mind about the nature of theology. It was the 1992 Democratic Convention, and Bill Clinton was delivering his acceptance speech, in effect dawning the mantle of party leadership as they moved into the fall election. At first, I noticed only the "New Covenant" section of the speech, somewhere near the middle, and thought it was an interesting choice, a good way of signaling both the sacred origins of the nation as well as a theme of a new beginning. Had not the Pilgrims spoken in similar terms of a "compact?" This "New Covenant" was an interesting move, a return of sorts to that early political starting point, but also letting Republicans know that Democrats would not be surrendering the religious/moral-values ground to groups like the Christian Coalition and Jerry Falwell's Moral Majority.

It would be some months later before I looked at the speech more carefully and noticed that Clinton's reference to the New Covenant had come directly in the middle of the speech. I began to wonder how he had set up that particular move. I then noticed that in the section directly before his proposal for a New Covenant Clinton had been speaking of the country "falling behind" under President Bush, who himself was caught up in "a failed economic theory." Clinton augmented this indictment of Bush's failure to lead with images of both sloth and arrogance—of not doing enough to help American workers and of being out of touch with the obligation to nurture the growth of the middle class.

"So, that's why we needed a New Covenant," I thought to myself. "But surely there hadn't been a downward slide all along." So, I turned to the beginning of the speech, and suddenly, as a theological reader, I knew exactly where I was. Once the opening formalities of the speech were out of the way, Clinton began to locate himself, his character, and his policy proposals within the good and enduring values of his family, which were themselves expressions of the values of the "American Dream of an expanding middle class." He began with stories of his mother, his grandfather, and his wife, Hillary, whose concern for their family, their neighbors, and all of our children grounded his policy commitments. Yes, he argued, here was the starting point of the enduring goodness of the American people, a goodness not yet lost entirely, but needing a new advocate in the person of Bill Clinton to restore that goodness to the institutions of American political and economic life.

Once I saw the arc of these first three moves of the speech, I then turned to the latter sections with greater expectation. Clinton did not disappoint. For even in the process of concluding his proposal of the New Covenant between the government and its citizens, he sounded the theme of a revitalized community: words not only of union and community—"there is no 'them'; there is only us, one nation under God, indivisible with unity and justice for all"—but words also of "faith" and his castigation of then President Bush for mocking his [Clinton's] use of what Bush had called "the vision thing." I will dwell on only one significant passage about this new community that Clinton claimed would follow if he were elected and his New Covenant proposals were approved.

> But the New Covenant is about more than opportunities and responsibilities for you and your families. It's also about our common community. Tonight, every one of you knows deep in your heart that we are too divided. It is time to heal America. And so we must say to every American: Look beyond the stereotypes that blind us. We need each other—all of us—we need each other. We don't have a person to waste, and yet for too long politicians have told the most of us that are doing all right that what's really wrong with America is the rest of us—"them." Them—the minorities. Them—the liberals. Them—the poor. Them—the homeless. Them—the people with disabilities. Them—the gays. We've gotten to where we've nearly "themed" ourselves to death: Them, and them, and them. But, this is America. There is no "them." There is only "us." One nation, under God, indivisible, with liberty and justice for all. That—that, is our Pledge of Allegiance, and that's what the New Covenant is all about.

It is a remarkable passage in which the only "them" that remains are those who are doing the "theming"! The passage thus constructs a movement toward an inclusive and welcoming society even as it brilliantly critiques, with language both old and new, a position that no longer squares with the vision of society set forth in the New Covenant.

Appendix II: "Why Are These the Topics?" 101

But Clinton was not yet finished. In another move, focused on the language of vision for the future, he spoke as a father about his daughter, Chelsea, and the world she will inhabit.

> I want every person in this hall and every person in this land to reach out and join us in a great new adventure, to chart a bold new future.
>
> And then, as a student at Georgetown I heard that call clarified by a professor name Carol Quigley, who said to us that America was the greatest nation in history because our people had always believed in two things: that tomorrow can be better than today and that every one of us has a personal moral responsibility to make it so.
>
> That—that kind of future entered my life the night our daughter, Chelsea, was born. As I stood in the delivery room, I was overcome with the thought that God had given me a blessing my own father never knew—the chance to hold my child in my arms.
>
> Somewhere at this very moment a child is being born in America. Let it be our cause to give that child a happy home, a healthy family, and a hopeful future. Let it be our cause to see that that child has a chance to live to the fullest of her God-given capacities.
>
> Let it be—Let it be our cause to see that child grow up strong and secure, braced by her challenges but never struggling alone, with family and friends and a faith that, in America, no one is left out; no one is left behind.
>
> Let it be—Let it be our cause that when this child is able, she gives something back to her children, her community, and her country.
>
> Let it be our cause that we give this child a country that is coming together, not coming apart, a country of boundless hopes and endless dreams, a country that once again lifts its people and inspires the world. Let that be our cause, our commitment, and our New Covenant.
>
> My fellow Americans, I end tonight where it all began for me. I still believe in a place called Hope.

As Clinton had spoken of his mother, grandfather, and spouse at the beginning of the speech, linking their virtues to his learning, he turns at the end to speak of his daughter, Chelsea, and of the way she, and all our children, guide our sense of responsibility to provide for a future in which they can grow and thrive in an expanding vision of the American Dream.

When I had watched the speech the night of the convention, those moves had simply washed over me. Yes, I had caught the "New Covenant" theme, but the more subtle structure of the speech had gone unnoticed, and, I should say, by professional critics as well. One critic, writing in *The New York Times*, called attention to some of the rhetorical flourishes of the speech, but had failed to comment on any broader structure. Months later as I finished poring over the text of the speech, I was stunned that this speech, delivered in the act of donning the mantle of party leadership in the 1992 campaign for the presidency, should echo so closely the major topics that I was typically dealing with as a theologian: (1) creation in the Image of God; (2) Sin; (3) Redemption; (4) the Church, and (5) future vision or Eschatology. To be clear, I am not saying that Clinton was a theologian, but that the coherence of his proposal for leading the nation is analogous to the moves of a theological proposal.

Let's look at this notion of coherence more closely. Simply put, the way Clinton interpreted the goodness of the American people in that first topic would shape the way the second topic dealt with what was wrong in the Bush presidency. Because Clinton linked the goodness of America and the American Dream with an expanding middle class that is generous and fair and "plays by the rules," his sharpest criticism of President Bush was that his policies had undercut the middle class and thereby threatened the moral character of the nation itself. In order to persuade Americans to vote Bush out of office, Clinton had to argue not simply that Bush had made a few policy errors, which could, after all, be forgiven, but that Bush, while being a good man, was leading the country into social and moral disaster.

Clinton's speech needed to articulate a sense of urgency that the goodness and strength of America was being undermined by a leader who was not committed to strengthening and expanding the well-being of the American middle class. That is why Clinton's third topic announced what he called a New Covenant, a new understanding of the relationship between government and the people that restores the commitment to America's middle class, so recklessly threatened by Bush's policies. The country, Clinton argued, needed this New Covenant, and the only way to secure it would be by electing him.

From that pivotal moment in the speech—it was by far its longest section—Clinton then, as we have seen, affirmed the kind of community (topic four) that would follow from his election: an American community that would be less divisive, that would pull together to enhance all our fortunes collectively. That renewal of American community, authorized along the lines of his New Covenant, would in turn open a hopeful future (topic five) keeping the American Dream alive.

Appendix II: "Why Are These the Topics?"

If Clinton failed to connect these topics in a seamless way—and many political speeches fail to do so—then his speech would have lacked not only coherence but urgency, because it would have been unclear what he was asking the nation to choose between and why. And without coherence and urgency, Clinton's proposal would have also lacked persuasiveness. The way a proposal interprets one topic shapes the way it deals with the others.

For some years, I thought Clinton was simply a very bright fellow, using the topical structure of Christian theology to enhance and deepen the appeal of his candidacy. Indeed, numerous Christian theologians have written persuasively on how political discourse, particularly in America, has long drawn upon the themes of Christian theology.[2] Still, I was surprised to see this structure played out from beginning to end not only in Clinton's convention address but in others' as well.[3] Not all as eloquently to be sure, but the interactive flow of their speeches moving through those topics provided something of a common structure for their differing political proposals.

I had been so influenced by my teachers to see that political speech frequently plays off Christian, religious discourse to reach a wider audience that I was slow to imagine something else: what if the structure of Christian theology were itself inherently political? What if it was more fluid, more open to change than a static, fixed discourse? What if those Christian topics, instead of being entirely unique, or *sui generis*, were themselves particular manifestations of a more fundamental linguistic practice, namely that of offering proposals for leadership in response to the call, the challenge of moving into a difficult future.

---

2. Marty, *Religion and Republic*, 77–94.

3. To be clear, the candidate from the party that lost the election, gave a similarly structured speech. This rhetorical structure of proposing is not simply about winning.

Appendix III

Note on Theopoetics and Rhetoric

You know the criticism: Rhetoric is a discourse with no disciplinary home of its own, completely "supplementary,"—adding only beauty, perhaps, or a certain "rouging," as Caputo says in his dismissal of strong theologies. "Suppose," Caputo wonders in his Introduction to *The Weakness of God*, "all the trouble theology causes to itself and to others is brought about by sitting in the window, 'all rouged up and powdered' waiting for a virile power to come striding by hoping to get lucky."[1] A muscular God for a muscular theology that is all just make-up and ornamentation, empty rhetoric, and no genuine heart.

It is Caputo's image of strong theology going a whoring after "strong" gods, that conjures the easy dismissal of rhetoric as mere ornamentation. For that is the modern view of rhetoric—a surface discourse that "polishes the apple," as it were, while adding no real content. Derrida, however, writing of "the supplement," in *Of Grammatology*, notes that that which is supposedly supplementary to something else—the way writing, for example, is traditionally viewed as supplementary to the alleged, more complete presence of speech, is actually necessary to it. As one critic puts it:

> Derrida re-reads the texts of Rousseau and finds in them other irreducible and dangerous supplements: harmony as the supplement of melody, masturbation as the supplement of sexual relations, linguistic articulation as the supplement of voiced accent,

---

1. Caputo, *The Weakness of God*, 8

Appendix III: Note on Theopoetics and Rhetoric

education as the supplement of maternal nature, need as the supplement of passion, etc.

Although what is offered as a supplement changes, the 'logic' and the processes of supplementing remain the same: that which is seen as a supplement adds itself to a seemingly full, complete, pure, simple, original, self-sufficient, and self-contained presence, only to reveal, expose, or render apparent an absence, occurring as lacks and differences, residing in the origin of what seems complete and full and rendering possible its taking place in the first place.[2]

With Derrida we can ask, "what if rhetoric is not simply ornamentation?" What if rhetoric is the supplement of Caputo's poetics, adding itself "to a seemingly full, complete, pure, simple, original, self-sufficient" discourse?

---

2. See Aukhadra, "Derrida on Supplement and Supplementary."

Bibliography

Augustine, St. *Confessions*. Translated by John K. Ryan. New York: Doubleday, 1960.
———. *De doctrina christiana*. Translated by D. W. Robertson, Jr. New York: Macmillan/Library of Liberal Arts, 1958.
Aukhadra, Haitham. "Derrida on Supplement and Supplementary." Website *that–which*. https://that-which.com/derrida-on-supplement-and-supplementarity/. 2024.
Bessler, Joseph A. "Moving Words: The Political Life of Theology." *Fourth R* 33.5 (2022) 3–7, 22.
———. *A Scandalous Jesus: How Three Historic Quests Changed Theology for the Better*. Salem, OR: Polebridge, 2013.
Biesecker, Barbara. *Addressing Postmodernity: Kenneth Burke, Rhetoric, and a Theory of Social Change*. Tuscaloosa: University of Alabama Press, 1997.
———. "From General History to Philosophy: Black Lives Matter, Late Neoliberal Molecular Biopolitics, and Rhetoric." *Philosophy and Rhetoric* 50.4 (2017) 409–30.
———. "Rethinking the Rhetorical Situation from within the Thematic of *Différance*." *Philosophy and Rhetoric* 22.2 (1989) 232–46.
Caputo, John D. *Against Ethics: Contributions to a Poetics of Obligation with Constant reference to Deconstruction*. Studies in Continental Thought. Bloomington: Indiana University Press, 1993.
———. *Cross and Cosmos: A Theology of Difficult Glory*. Indiana Series in the Philosophy of Religion. Bloomington: Indiana University Press, 2019.
———. *Deconstruction in a Nutshell: A Conversation with Jacques Derrida*. Perspectives in Continental Philosophy 1. New York: Fordham University Press, 1997.
———. *The Folly of God: A Theology of the Unconditional*. Salem, OR: Polebridge, 2016.
———. *Hermeneutics: Facts and Interpretation in the Age of Information*. New York: Penguin, 2018.
———. *How to Read Kierkegaard*. How to Read. New York: Norton, 2007.
———. *The Insistence of God: A Theology of Perhaps*. Indiana Series in the Philosophy of Religion. Bloomington: Indiana University Press, 2013.

———. *The Mystical Element in Heidegger's Thought*. Rev. reprint. New York: Fordham University Press, 1986.

———. *The Prayers and Tears of Jacques Derrida: Religion without Religion*. Indiana Series in the Philosophy of Religion. Bloomington: Indiana University Press, 1997.

———. *Radical Hermeneutics: Repetition, Deconstruction, and the Hermeneutic Project*. Studies in Phenomenology and Existential Philosophy. Bloomington: Indiana University Press, 1987.

———. "A Short Precis of *The Weakness of God* and *The Insistence of God*." *Forum*, third series 5,2 (Fall 2016) 107–17.

———. *Specters of God: An Anatomy of the Apophatic Imagination*. Bloomington: Indiana University Press, 2022.

———. "The Time of America." In *Doing Theology in the Age of Trump: A Critical Report on Christian Nationalism*, edited by Jeffrey W. Robbins and Clayton Crockett, 77–81. Eugene, OR: Cascade Books, 2018.

———. *Truth: Philosophy in Transit*. New York: Penguin, 2013.

———. *The Weakness of God: A Theology of the Event*. Indiana Series in the Philosophy of Religion. Bloomington: Indiana University Press, 2006.

———. *What to Believe? Twelve Brief Lessons in Radical Theology*. New York: Columbia University Press, 2023.

———. *What Would Jesus Deconstruct?* Grand Rapids: Baker Academic, 2007.

Caputo, John D., and Michael J. Scanlon, eds. *Augustine and Postmodernism*. Bloomington: Indiana University Press, 2005.

Chopp, Rebecca. "Theology and the Poetics of Testimony." In *Converging on Culture: Theologians in Dialogue with Cultural Analysis and Criticism*. edited by Delwin Brown, Sheila Grave Davaney, and Kathryn Tanner, 56–70. Oxford: Oxford University Press, 2001.

Clinton, William Jefferson. "Democratic Presidential Nomination Acceptance Address." *American Rhetoric Online Speech Bank*. https://www.americanrhetoric.com/speeches/wjclinton1992dnc.htm.

Compier, Don. *What Is Rhetorical Theology? Textual Practice and Public Discourse*. Harrisburg, PA: Trinity, 1999.

Crockett, Clayton. *Derrida After the End of Writing: Political Theology and New Materialism*. Perspectives in Continental Philosophy. New York: Fordham University Press, 2017.

Crossan, John Dominic. *Jesus: A Revolutionary Biography*. San Francisco: HarperSanFrancisco, 1995.

Davis, Diane. *Inessential Solidarity: Rhetoric and Foreigner Relations*. Pittsburgh: University of Pittsburgh Press, 2010.

———. "Addressing Alterity: Rhetoric, Hermeneutics and the Nonappropriative Relation." *Philosophy and Rhetoric* 38.3 (2005) 191–212.

Derrida, Jacques. *Acts of Religion*. Edited by Gil Anidjar. New York: Routledge, 2002.

———. *Margins of Philosophy*. Translated by Alan Bass. Chicago: University of Chicago Press, 1982.

———. *Of Grammatology*. Translated by Gayatri Chakravorty Spivak. Corrected ed. Baltimore: Johns Hopkins University Press, 1998.

Dooley, Mark. "From Radical Hermeneutics to the *Weakness* of God: John D. Caputo in Dialogue with Mark Dooley." Edited by Ian Leask. *Philosophy Today* 51.2. (2007) 216–26.

———, ed. *A Passion for the Impossible: John D. Caputo in Focus*. Albany: State University of New York Press, 2003.
Doxtader, Erik, ed. *Inventing the Potential of Rhetorical Culture: The Works and Legacy of Thomas B. Farrell*. University Park: Pennsylvania State University Press, 2009.
Farrell, Thomas B., ed. *Landmark Essays on Contemporary Rhetoric*. Landmark Essays 15. Mahwah, NJ: Erlbaum, 1998.
———. *Norms of Rhetorical Culture*. New Haven: Yale University Press, 1993.
———. "The Weight of Rhetoric: Studies in Cultural Delirium." *Philosophy and Rhetoric* 41.4. (2008) 467–87.
Foss, Sonja K., and Cindy L. Griffin. "Beyond Persuasion: A Proposal for an Invitational Rhetoric." *Communications Monographs* 62 (1995) 2–8.
Funk, Robert, and Roy Hoover, and the Jesus Seminar. *The Five Gospels*. New York: HarperCollins, 1993.
Gaonkar, Dilip Parameshwar. "Rhetoric and Its Double: Reflections on the Rhetorical Turn in the Human Sciences." In *Contemporary Rhetorical Theory*, edited by John Louis Lucaites et al., 341–66. New York: Guilford, 1999.
Gross, Daniel, and Ansgar Kemmann, eds. *Heidegger and Rhetoric*. SUNY Series in Contemporary Continental Philosophy. Albany: State University of New York Press, 2005.
———. *Being-Moved: Rhetoric as the Art of Listening*. Rhetoric and Public Culture. Oakland: University of California Press, 2020.
Heaney, Seamus. "Crediting Poetry." The Nobel Lecture. In *Opened Ground: Selected Poems 1966–1996*. New York: Farrar, Straus & Giroux, 1998.
Hyde, Michael. *The Call of Conscience: Heidegger, Levinas, Rhetoric and the Euthanasia Debate*. Studies in Rhetoric/Communication. Columbia: University of South Carolina Press, 2001.
Keller, Catherine. Review of *Weakness of God*, by John D. Caputo. *Crosscurrents* (Winter 2007) 133–39.
Kierkegaard, Søren. *Concluding Unscientific Postscript*. Translated by David E. Swenson and Walter Lowrie. Princeton: Princeton University Press, 1941.
Lakoff, George, and Mark Johnson. *Metaphors We Live By*. Chicago: University of Chicago Press, 1980.
———. *Moral Politics: How Liberals and Conservatives Think*. New York: Penguin, 1996.
Lakoff, George, and Mark Turner. *More Than Cool Reason: A Field Guide to Poetic Metaphor*. Chicago: University of Chicago Press, 1989.
Leff, Michael. "Hermeneutical Rhetoric." In *Rethinking Rhetorical Theory, Criticism, and Pedagogy: The Living Art of Michael C. Leff*, edited by Antonio de Velasco et al. East Lansing: Michigan State University Press, 2016.
Lunsford, Andrea A., and John J. Ruszkiewicz. *Everything's an Argument*. Boston: Bedford/St. Martin's, 2013.
Mailloux, Stephen. "Rhetorical Hermeneutics." *Critical Inquiry* 11.4 (1985) 620–41.
Marty, Martin E. *Religion and Republic*. Boston: Beacon, 1987.
Matthews. Gary. "Conceit in Literature: Concept & Examples." https://study.com/academy/lesson/conceit-in-literature-definition-examples-quiz.html.
Meyer, Michael. ed. *From Metaphysics to Rhetoric*. Translated by Robert Harvey. Synthese Library 202. Dordrecht: Kluwer Academic, 1989.

Olson, Gary A. "Jacques Derrida on Rhetoric and Composition: A Conversation." *Journal of Advanced Composition*. 10.1 (1990) 1–21.

Parrott, John B. "George Lakoff's New Happiness: Politics after Rationality." *Academic Quest* 22 (2009) 414–30.

Plato. *The Republic*. Translated by G. M. A. Grub. Indianapolis: Hackett, 1992.

Putt, B. Keith. "Reconciling Pure Forgiveness and Reconciliation: Bringing John Caputo into the Kingdom of God." *CrossCurrents* 59 (2009) 500–539.

Ricoeur, Paul. "Rhetoric—Poetics—Hermeneutics." In *From Metaphysics to Rhetoric*, edited by Michael Meyer, 137–50. Synthese Library 202. Dordrecht: Kluwer Academic, 1989.

Rieger, Michael Joseph. "Figuring the Topos: Finding Common Ground in Cognitive Environments." *Philosophy and Rhetoric* 57.1 (2024) 30–53.

Robbins, Jeffrey W., and Clayton Crockett, eds. *Doing Theology in the Age of Trump: A Critical Report on Christian Nationalism*. Eugene, OR: Cascade Books, 2018.

———. Review of *The European Reception of John D. Caputo's Thought: Radicalizing Theology*. in Joeri Schrijvers and Martin Koci, eds. *Journal for Continental Philosophy of Religion*. (2024) 1–3.

Rollins, Brooke. "Persuasion's Ethical Force: Levinas and Gorgias and the Rhetorical Address." *JAC* 29.3 (2009) 539–59.

Schrijvers, Joeri, and Martin Koci, eds. *The European Reception of John D. Caputo's Thought: Radicalizing Theology*. Lanham, MD: Lexington, 2023.

Smith, Craig R. *Rhetoric and Human Consciousness: A History*. 4th ed. Long Grove, IL: Waveland, 2013.

Sokoloff, William J. "Between Justice and Legality Derrida on Decision." *Political Research Quarterly* 58.2 (2005) 341–52.

Theoharis, Jeanne. "Rosa Parks's Transformative Two Weeks at the Highlander Research and Education Center." Beacon Broadside: A Project of Beacon Press. April 9, 2019.

Tillich, Paul. *On the Boundary: An Autobiographical Sketch*. New York: Scribner, 1966

Ure, Michael. "Foucault's Rhetorical Practice: The 1961 Preface to History and Madness." *Philosophy and Rhetoric* 56.2 (2023).

Zlomislić, Marko, and Neal DeRoo, eds. *Cross and Khôra: Deconstruction and Christianity in the Work of John D. Caputo*. Postmodern Ethics Series 1. Eugene, OR: Pickwick Publications, 2010.

Index

action, 5, 17, 34, 44, 45, 47, 54–55, 61, 65, 67–68, 83, 86, 91, 94. *See also* call; faith
Against Ethics (Caputo), 35, 41, 51, 83
America/American people, 17, 20, 65–66, 99–103
appearances, 10, 16, 21–23
argument/argumentation, 5, 11, 13, 15, 18, 21–23, 27–28, 31, 33, 37–38, 41–42, 80, 89, 94. *See also* debate; proposals; rhetoric/rhetorical
Aristotle, 5, 16, 18, 46–47
audiences, 1–2, 9–13, 19, 20–21, 23, 33–34, 38, 45–46, 49, 50, 56–57, 68, 87, 89, 97. *See also* readers
Augustine, St., 23, 31–32, 36, 52, 88–91, 89n4
Augustine and Postmodernism, 45
authority, 2, 14–15, 32–34, 32n9, 42, 50, 87, 89, 91, 96

Barth, Karl, 37
becoming true, 15. See also *facere veritatem*
being. *See* presence
being moved, 4, 18, 29, 34, 51–52, 58, 61, 71, 89–90, 89n4. *See also* feeling; persuasion; transformation

Being Moved (Gross), 45
belief, 17, 21, 50, 52–53, 60, 63, 68–71, 75, 80
Bible, 24–29, 31n5, 40–42, 50–52, 70. *See also* kingdom/Kingdom of God; miracles; parables; Scriptures
Biesecker, Barbara, 4–5, 23
Bitzer, Lloyd, 2
boundary/boundaries, 15, 26, 43, 60, 66
Burke, Kenneth, 11, 14

call, 1–5, 13, 15, 24–29, 56–60
being called, 4, 41, 43, 49, 52n14, 54, 65
call and response, 30–34, 43–44, 45, 49–50, 52–54, 66–68, 70–73
call without a caller, 50–51, 87
cosmopoetics, 72–75
event of, 14, 32–33, 43, 49, 52–53, 61
existentialism, 53–54
and "God," 77–78
and interruption, 94n5
invitational rhetoric, 49–52
life, gift of, 75–77
movement of readers, 89
of the other, 61–63
and *phronesis*, 45
political speech(es), 23
preoriginary, 82–87

call (*cont.*)
    priority of the reader, 35–37
    and response, 81–87
    as rhetorical phenomenon, 81
    rhetoric and argumentation, 94
    to transformation, 17–19, 22n34
capacity, 15, 42, 47, 57, 60–63, 65, 77, 83
certainty, 2, 4, 12, 15, 17–18, 21–23, 31, 36, 40, 45, 59–60, 78–79, 96–97. *See also* logic
chiasmic call and response, 45, 66–67, 71–73
Chopp, Rebecca, 94
Christianity, 2, 11–13, 21, 31n5, 56–58, 64, 72, 77–79, 91
Christology, 65–68, 98–99
church, 68–73
Cicero, 11, 28n10, 90
Climacus, 38
Clinton, William Jefferson, 99–103
comparative standards, 37–38
Compier, Don, 11, 18–19, 52, 90
confessional theologies, 19, 58, 63–65, 66–67, 68–71, 75–77
Confessions (Augustine), 31–32, 36, 87, 88–91, 89n4
conventionality, 12, 15, 17, 55, 62, 65, 79, 95
coram Deo (before God), 31–32, 34, 37, 89
cosmopoetics, 72–75
courage, 15, 22–23, 54, 60, 61, 63, 66, 68, 77, 94. *See also* action; faith
cross, 10, 13, 19, 66. *See also* foolishness; Paul, the Apostle; suffering; wisdom
Crossan, John Dominic, 54–55

Davis, Diane, 80–87
death of the author, 32n9, 50
debate, 5, 26–28, 33, 37, 39–40, 45, 54, 80. *See also* argument/argumentation; proposals; rhetoric/rhetorical
deconstruction, 22n34, 46, 77–79
De doctrina christiana (Augustine), 90
democracy, 15, 49n5

Derrida, Jacques, 5n12, 22n34, 28, 32–33, 33–34, 39–41, 45, 69, 77–79, 93–94, 104–5. *See also* gift
Dewey, Arthur J., 25
discourse, 1–5, 15
    cosmopoetics, 72–75
    and hermeneutics, 34, 94
    and *phronesis*, 47
    and politics, 16–17, 57, 95, 103
    proposal-type discourse, 56–57
    public discourse, 28n10, 37, 56, 90, 97
    and readers, 35
    and rhetoric, 23, 94, 104–5
    saying and the said, 81–82, 85
    of theology, 46, 89–90
    weak theology, 40
    See also response/responsiveness

Eckhart, Meister, 23, 70, 76
empire, 10–11, 15, 27
eschatology, 75–77
eschaton, 58
essence, 62, 84
ethics, 43, 46, 51, 76, 83–84
event(s), 1–3, 14, 22, 22n34, 28, 32–33, 35–36, 43, 48–50, 52–53, 60–63, 66–67, 71–72, 76, 78, 84–86. *See also* call
"Everyday Language and Rhetoric Without Eloquence" (Lévinas), 83
Everything's an Argument (Lunsford and Ruszkiewicz), 56–57
existence, 4, 31n5, 32n9, 35, 53–54, 66–67, 69–70, 73, 85
existentialism, 53–54
experience, 4, 30, 32, 35–37, 41–42, 49–50, 67–68, 77, 89–90

face, 82–84, 87. *See also* Lévinas, Emmanuel
facere veritatem, 44n15, 50. *See also* becoming true
faith, 17–18, 21, 51, 52, 56, 60, 63, 68, 70–71, 76–77, 83, 89, 98, 100. *See also* action; courage

Index

Farrell, Thomas B., 2, 12–13, 16, 20–22, 25, 30–31, 34, 40, 44–46, 51, 54, 68. *See also* magnitude; matter; weight

feeling, 41, 88–89. *See also* being moved; courage; heart; longing(s)

feminist theology, 9–10

The Five Gospels (Funk), 54–55

foolishness, 10, 13, 19, 43. *See also* cross; Paul, the Apostle; wisdom

"The Force of Law" (Derrida), 78–79

Foss, Sonja K., 49

Foucault, Michel, xiii, 49–50

Funk, Robert, 54–55

Gadamer, Hans Georg, 40, 93. *See also* Heidegger, Martin; hermeneutics

Gaonkar, Dilip Parameshwar, 3–4, 23

gathering, 70

gift, 17, 33–34, 64, 69, 74, 75–77, 89

Gingrich, Newt, 16

God, 9–13, 15, 17, 31–33, 57–60, 61–63, 66–67, 68–74, 75–77, 77–79, 85–87, 89–91. *See also* kingdom/Kingdom of God; strong force; weakness/weak force

Goldwater, Barry, 14

grace, 64, 76

Griffin, Cindy L., 49

Gross, Daniel, 45, 47

hard arguments, 13, 15. *See also* argument/argumentation

Heaney, Seamus, 94

heart, 5, 14, 21, 34, 37, 41–43, 46, 53–55, 68
  hardness of, 23, 25–27, 33, 51–52, 55, 65
  See also courage; faith

Hegel, Georg Wilhelm Friedrich, 38

Heidegger, Martin, 38n27, 47, 64, 75, 93. *See also* existentialism; Gadamer, Hans Georg; hermeneutics

Heidegger and Rhetoric (Gross), 47

hermeneutics, 14, 34, 44–46, 55, 56, 80–87, 93–97. *See also* existentialism; Gadamer, Hans Georg; Heidegger, Martin

Highlander Folk School's Research and Education Center, 22

honour, 16

Horton, Myles, 22

hospitality, 18, 37n24, 60–63, 70, 73–75, 91

hostipitality, 61

How to Read Kierkegaard (Caputo), 11n3, 30–34

human/non-human world, 72–74

humility, 15, 59–60, 74–75, 93

hyperbole, 11, 18, 28n13. *See also* tropes/tropical

hyper-realism, 15

image/image-clusters, 13, 14–18, 28n13, 31, 33, 52, 78. *See also* face

imagination, 15

Imago Dei, 62

impossible/impossibility, 4, 10, 13, 22, 22n34, 33, 61–63, 85, 91

incarnation, 66–67

Inessential Solidarity (Davis), 80–87

insistence, 60, 62, 66–67, 69–70, 73, 75

The Insistence of God (Caputo), 5, 48, 58, 65, 70–72, 83

interpretation, 18, 35, 37, 46, 50, 55, 56, 58–59, 65, 68, 69, 81, 83, 96–97

interruption, 13, 17, 19–23, 36, 61–62, 79, 81–82, 83, 85–86, 94, 94n5

invitation/invitational rhetoric, 15, 19, 24, 32–33, 35–37, 43, 48–54, 58, 78, 83. *See also* luring

inwardness, Kierkegaard's emphasis on, 37–38

Jackson, Jesse, 20–22

Jesus, 13, 21, 23, 25–28, 43–44, 50, 55, 57–58, 66, 68, 70, 78, 81–82, 85

Jesus (Crossan), 55

Johnson, Mark, 14, 95

justice, 2–3, 15, 17, 22–23, 24–27, 38, 43–44, 69–71, 78–79. *See also* kingdom/Kingdom of God

kardia, 3, 14, 27, 37–38, 41–43, 46–47, 68

Kearney, Richard, 45

Keller, Catherine, 9–10, 23, 52

Kennedy, Robert F., 23, 90n6

Kierkegaard, Søren, 11n3, 29, 30–38, 52, 55, 69
kinesis, 47
King, Martin Luther Jr., 65–66
kingdom/Kingdom of God, 10, 13, 15, 37n24, 43–44, 50, 68, 78–79, 81–82, 85–86, 91. *See also* Bible; God; justice; miracles; parables; Scriptures
Kock, Christian, 5
krisis, 43, 44–45
Kuhn, Thomas, 3–4

Lakoff, George, 14, 16–17, 95–96
law, 15, 24–27, 54, 78–79. *See also* justice; strong force
Lebensraum, 19, 83. *See also* worldview(s)
Lentriccia, Frank, 52
Lévinas, Emmanuel, 5n12, 36–38, 80–87, 93. *See also* Davis, Diane; face
liberal politics, 16–17
life, gift of, 17, 74, 75–77
Lincoln, Abraham, 23, 97
logic, 5, 18, 23, 66–67, 70, 75, 77–78, 93–94. *See also* certainty
logos, 5, 27, 41–42, 46, 47, 79
longing(s), 18, 33, 33n11, 42, 76, 89, 90–91. *See also* feeling; prayers
Lunsford, Andrea A., 56–57
luring, 4, 13, 15, 19, 35, 40, 49, 54, 59, 66–67, 77–78. *See also* invitation/invitational rhetoric; persuasion

magnitude, 12, 31, 38. *See also* Farrell, Thomas B.; matter; weight
Mailloux, Stephen, 81, 96–97. *See also* Davis, Diane; hermeneutics; rhetoric/rhetorical
"A Man with a Withered Hand," 24–27, 40–42
margins, 1–2, 19–21, 24, 34, 44, 68
Mark, Gospel of, 24–27, 40–42. *See also* miracles; Pharisees/religious leaders
Martha (sister of Lazarus), 70, 73–74
Mary (mother of Jesus), 67

Mary (sister of Lazarus), 70
matter, 2, 12–13, 54, 61, 72
Matthew, Gospel of, 68–69
Matthews, Ian, 88–89
metanoia/metanoetics, 4, 17–18, 42–43, 46–47, 89. *See also* poetics; theopoetics
metaphors, 14, 16–18, 28, 47, 88, 95. *See also* tropes/tropical
Metaphors We Live By (Lakoff and Johnson), 14, 95–96
Metz, J. B., 38n27
"Michel Foucault's Rhetorical Practice" (Ure), 49–50
miracles, 25–27. *See also* Mark, Gospel of; Pharisees/religious leaders
models of the family, 16–17
modernity, 36–37, 67
Montgomery Bus Boycott, 22–23
Moral Politics (Lakoff), 16–17, 95
moral systems, 17
movement/motion, 3–5, 17–19, 21–23, 28–29, 34, 37, 47, 56–60, 62, 79, 89–90. *See also* being moved; persuasion; poetics; rhetoric/rhetorical; transformation
The Mystical Element in Heidegger's Thought (Caputo), 64

Nancy, Jean Luc, 86
natality, 62
nature/naturalism, 72–74, 96–97
negative capability, 62
Neo-Platonism, 89n4, 91
Nietzsche, Friedrich, 30, 46
non-hermeneutical dimension of rhetoric, 81–82
non-violence, 15, 28n10
Norms of Rhetorical Culture (Farrell), 20–21
nous, 14, 27–28, 41–42, 43, 47

obligation, 30, 35, 41, 51, 55, 81–87, 95–96
Of Grammatology (Derrida), 104
Olson, Gary A., xii
omnipotence, 11–13, 17–18

onomatopoeia, 54. *See also* tropes/
    tropical
open debate, 39–40
oratory, 23
other, 33, 41–42, 43, 51–52, 61–63. *See
    also* self

parables, 13, 18, 21, 28, 47, 67
Parks, Rosa, 22–23
pathos and *ethos*, 5, 28, 47
Paul, the Apostle, 10, 13, 19, 72. *See also*
    cross; foolishness; wisdom
perhaps, 4, 19, 35, 49–51, 59–60, 62,
    66–67, 69. *See also* suppose
persuasion, 4, 14, 19, 23, 28, 30, 34–38,
    52, 54, 56–58, 68, 71, 89–90,
    97, 102–3. *See also* argument/
    argumentation; debate;
    invitation/invitational rhetoric;
    luring; rhetoric/rhetorical;
    weakness/weak force
Pharisees/religious leaders, 25–27. *See
    also* Mark, Gospel of
philosophy, xiii, 27–28, 38, 59, 78,
    80–82, 84, 91, 93
Philosophy and Rhetoric (journal), 5
phronesis, 41–47
Plato, 10, 52n14
poetics, 4, 28, 47, 50, 56, 58, 66–67,
    69, 76, 86, 93–97, 105. *See
    also metanoia/metanoetics;*
    movement/motion; theopoetics
polemic/polemical, 11, 16, 26, 40,
    49, 69. *See also* argument/
    argumentation; debate
political and theological, 2, 63
political discourse, 16–17, 57, 95, 103
political life, 40
political speech(es), 23, 99–103
politics of sovereignty, 77–78
power, 1–2, 9–13, 14, 16–18, 21, 24–26,
    30–31, 44, 46, 48–49, 68, 77–79,
    89–90, 97. *See also* sovereignty;
    strong force; weakness/weak
    force
prayers, 4, 15, 76–77, 89–91. *See also*
    feeling; longing(s); response/
    responsiveness

preoriginary call, 82–87
presence, 11–12, 15, 48, 66, 77, 93
pride, 64, 66
priority, 15, 34, 35, 38, 43, 51, 70, 81, 84
proposals, 1–5, 27–28
    and Christology, 65–68
    Derrida's Law/Justice dynamic,
        78–79
    development of the theopoetic
        proposal, 56–60
    and "God," 77–78
    invitation/invitational rhetoric, 49,
        51–52, 83
    New Covenant proposals, Clinton's,
        99–103
    Paul, the Apostle, 10
    and *phronesis*, 42
    See also argument/argumentation;
        debate; rhetoric/rhetorical
pseudonymous authors, 30–32, 35–37

radical hermeneutics, 56, 96–97
Radical Hermeneutics (Caputo), 39–40,
    44
radical theology, 15, 44, 54, 58, 63,
    64–65, 69–73, 76
Rahner, Karl, 38n27
readers, 30–38, 45–46, 48–52, 52–54,
    85, 88–91
Reagan, Ronald, 14, 20
realism, 60, 65, 74, 77, 96–97
reduction, 84–85
refutative enthymeme, 20–22, 44–45
religion, 12, 48, 54, 69, 73–74, 76
religious authorship, 31–33, 34–35
repetition, 30, 94–95, 95n6
response/responsiveness, 15, 26–29,
    30–34, 36, 42, 43–44, 45, 49,
    52–54, 60–62, 63–64, 66–68,
    70–73, 81–86, 90, 94
revelation, 52–53. *See also* call
Rhetoric (Aristotle), 16, 47
"The Rhetorical Situation" (Bitzer), 2
Rhetoric and Human Consciousness
    (Smith), 14
rhetoric/rhetorical, 2–5, 5n12, 14, 27–29
    and appearances, 16
    and argumentation, 18

rhetoric/rhetorical (*cont.*)
    Augustine's *Confessions*, 88–91
    character of Caputo, 23
    Davis' approach to, 80–87
    dismissal of as ornamentation, 104–5
    and interruption, 94, 94n5
    invitational rhetoric, 32–33, 48–54, 83
    and Kierkegaard, 32–34, 37–38
    literary conceit, 88–89
    and *phronesis*, 45–46, 47
    poetics and hermeneutics, 93–97
    priority of audience in, 9–13
    proposal structure, 56–58
    and Scriptures, 53
    See also argument/argumentation; debate; persuasion; weakness/weak force
right belief, 13, 52–53, 60, 80
risk, 61–63
Rome, 10, 23
Roosevelt, Franklin Delano, 23
Rorty, Richard, 39
Ruszkiewicz, John J., 56–57

saying and the said, 81–86
Scriptures, 31n5, 50, 50n9, 52–53, 85–86. *See also* Bible; kingdom/Kingdom of God; miracles; parables
scrivener, 7, 13, 32n9. *See also* Kierkegaard, Søren
self, 15, 41, 43–44, 82
    self-protection, 1, 65
"A Short Precise of *The Weakness of God* and *The Insistence of God*" (Caputo), 47
sin, 64–68, 98, 102
Smith, Craig R., 14
social knowledge, 2, 97
social transformation, 4
Socrates, 10, 34–35
solidarity, 82
sovereignty, 12, 15, 42, 77–78. *See also* power; strong force
Specters of God (Caputo), 18, 44
status quo, 12
stranger, 60–63

"strong father" and "nurturant parent," 17, 96
strong force, 78
strong theology, 12–13, 28n10, 40–42
    abuses of, 56
    confessional theologies, 68–69
    Derrida's Law/Justice dynamic, 79
    dismissal of rhetoric as ornamentation, 104
    event of a call, 43
    invitational rhetoric, 48–49
    and Kierkegaard, 38
    movement of readers, 90–91
    movement of to weak theology, 14–19, 49, 79
    and *phronesis*, 44–46, 47
    and revelation, 52
    set of images and markers, 14–15
    and theopoetics, 27–28
The Structure of Scientific Revolutions (Kuhn), 3–4
suffering, 21, 22, 40–41, 51–52, 53–54, 65, 76–77
sui generis, 57, 103
supernaturalism, 18–19, 50n9, 96–97
suppose, 4, 19, 35, 48–49, 104

tears, 4, 15, 33, 76, 81, 89–90
tertium quid, 5
theologians to-come, 17, 65
theo-logic, 15, 21
theology, 1–5, 13, 38, 38n27, 54n20
    being claimed, 54
    Christian theology, 56–58
    classical theology, 65–66, 70
    confessional theologies, 19, 58, 63–65, 66–67, 68–71, 75–77
    modern theology, 49
    radical theology, 15, 44, 54, 58, 63, 64–65, 69–73, 76
    as theopoetics, 89–90
    See also strong theology; weak theology
Theology in the Age of Trump (Robbins and Crockett), 65–66
theopoetics, 3, 10, 15, 17–18, 21, 23, 27–28, 30, 34, 40, 44, 58, 66, 68, 70–79, 89–90

theopraxis, 44
theorists, 4, 96–97
theory, 93–97
Tillich, Paul, 60
Tindale, C. W., 2
transcendence/transcendent, 52, 62–63, 74, 82
transformation, 4, 17–19, 22n34, 34, 42–43, 49–52, 53–54, 57–59, 84–85, 89, 89n4
tropes/tropical, 27, 28n13, 38, 42, 47, 57, 78, 97
Trump, Donald J., 65–66
truth(s), 15, 31n2, 31n5, 35–37, 37n24, 42
   and authorship, 30–31
   call and response, 45
   confessional theologies, 64, 69–71
   dogmatic, 21, 24, 46, 52
   inability to set aside, 87
   poetics of the event, 50
   and repetition, 95n6
   and revelation, 52–53
   and uncertainty, 60
   See also becoming true; *facere veritatem*
two-worlds logic of classical theology, 65–66, 70, 75–76

uncertainty, 4, 12, 15, 19, 28, 35–37, 54, 59–62, 68. *See also* deconstruction; Derrida, Jacques; poetics; rhetoric/rhetorical
unconditionality, 2, 26, 30, 61, 77–78, 84, 91. *See also* call; revelation
undecidability, 46, 59, 60, 61–63
universe, 72–76
Ure, Michael, xiii, 49–50

Vatz, Richard, 2
violence, 15, 20–21, 28n10, 52, 56
vulnerability, 54

The Weakness of God (Caputo), 1–2, 5, 9–13, 24, 31, 40–44, 47, 48–50, 52–54, 83–87, 88–91, 104
weakness/weak force, 10–11, 13, 14–19, 21, 24, 28, 48, 52–55, 54, 70, 78, 86–87
weak theology, 1–2, 21
   call of the other, 42
   Derrida's Law/Justice dynamic, 79
   and Kierkegaard, 35–38
   movement of strong theology to, 14–19, 49, 79
   open debate, 40
   "parasitic character" of, 46, 69
   and persuasion, 28
   and *phronesis,* 46, 47
   priority of audience in rhetoric and, 9–13
   set of images and markers, 14–15
   uncertainty and vulnerability, 54
weight, 15, 31–33, 35. *See also* Farrell, Thomas B.; matter
"The Weight of Rhetoric: Studies in Cultural Delirium" (Farrell), 12
What Is Rhetorical Theology? (Compier), 52
What Would Jesus Deconstruct? (Caputo), 5, 32, 42–43, 46
White Mythology (Derrida), 28
wisdom, 10. *See also* foolishness; Paul, the Apostle; weakness/weak force
witness, 24, 53–54. *See also* action; call; courage; faith
worldview(s), 17, 64, 66, 78n61, 81, 85, 89, 91, 96. *See also Lebensraum*
writing and reading, 35, 86

www.ingramcontent.com/pod-product-compliance
Lightning Source LLC
Chambersburg PA
CBHW020855160426
43192CB00007B/936